TECHNOLOGY, ENVIRONMENT AND HUMAN VALUES

About the Editor

K.M. Mohapatra, M.A. (Economics) from Utkal University, and M. Phil and Ph. D (Economics) from Jawaharlal Nehru University, New Delhi, has served as a Lecturer (Economics) in Orissa Degree Colleges — at Balavoomi Mahavidyalaya, Avana, from 1982 to 1983, and at U.N. College, Soro, from 1983 to 1985. Since 1989, he has been a regular faculty in Economics at the Department of Humanities and Social Sciences, H.B.T.I., Kanpur, Uttar Pradesh.

Dr. Mohapatra has a better accomplishment in conducting research projects — as a Project Director in an ICSSR sponsored project and as a Co-investigator in an Indo-Canadian Partnership Project sponsored by SICI-CIDA, and also, in supervising Ph.D. scholars.

He has to his credit publication of a book, entitled *Exploitative Tenancy and Technological Backwardness in Indian Agriculture* and contribution of chapters to the edited books *Managing Environmental Risks* and *Detergents and the Environment — The Canadian Experience and Indian Scenario.*

Besides, he has published several research articles in reputed journals such as *Economic and Political Weekly, Indian Journal of Agricultural Economics* and *Orissa Economic Journal* and research papers in proceedings of many national and international conferences, seminars and symposia.

Environmental Economics is his current research area.

TECHNOLOGY, ENVIRONMENT AND HUMAN VALUES

(A Metaphysical Approach to Sustainable Development)

Edited by

K.M. Mohapatra

CONCEPT PUBLISHING COMPANY, NEW DELHI-110059

ISBN 81-8069-089-X

First Published 2004

Published and Printed by
Ashok Kumar Mittal
Concept Publishing Company
A/15-16, Commercial Block, Mohan Garden
New Delhi-110059 (INDIA)

Phones : 25351460, 25351794
Fax : 091-11-25357103
Email : publishing@conceptpub.com

Preface

Protection of human beings and their environment from the adversities of industrialisation and scientific and technological applications has become a burning issue all over the world. Scientific and technological developments in various fields have made the possibility of mass production and mass consumption. Due to their impacts, the human thoughts and desires have been rapidly changing towards excessive consumerism and materialism. The human becomes over-enthusiastic for the possession of power and wealth. Moral and ethical values, which rest at higher level of consciousness and rationality in human, have been deteriorating. All these factors make him highly selfish, myopic and self-centred. Owing to that, the sustainable development and stability of the social and the natural orders have become doubtful. This book seeks to address the above issues.

An earnest attempt is made to incorporate the contextual thoughts and opinions of many distinguished academicians and researchers culled from various institutions all over the country. It contains twenty-two essays, classified under four broad sections. Each section consists of five to six articles. The main theme of discussion is related to the issues how today's scientific and technological inventions in different fields of knowledge deviating from human value norms lead to cause adverse impacts on the quality of human living, environment and development, how to attach human values to technical and scientific discoveries so that their adversities can be minimized, and why a parallel development of both 'materialism' and 'spiritualism' is necessary in this context. Discussions in each section are highly thought-provoking and touching fundamentals of reality of life and development. Many studies are based on primary information.

No doubt, contents of this book will be highly useful for all sections of readers. From this book, scientists, technocrats, economists, researchers and policy-makers who directly involve in inventions and technology transfers, will get many insights towards their righteous actions and policy-decisions. Particularly, many titles of this book will comply with new course structure in humanity and social science subjects designed for engineering and technology students in Indian universities. Thus, this can be referred as text-book to engineering and technology students.

K.M. Mohapatra

Acknowledgements

I greatly feel pleasure to convey my gratitude to the following distinguished persons from whom I have received inspiration and help towards this effort.

I am ever indebted to my teacher Prof. G.K. Chadha, presently, Vice-chancellor of Jawaharlal Nehru Univeristy, New Delhi under whose advice and inspiration I continuously keep in touch with research and writing activities.

I am highly thankful to Prof. K.P. Singh, Director and Prof. V.K. Jain, Ex-Director, H.B.T.I. Kanpur; and Prof. S.G. Dhande, Director IIT, Kanpur. Prof. C.V.S.K. Rao and Prof. K.K. Ghosh of H.B.T.I. Kanpur; and Prof. B. Rath and Prof. R. Saran of IIT Kanpur, for their inspiration and help at different stages for preparing this book.

I am equally thankful to Prof. Raka Saran, Dept. of HSS, IIT Kanpur and in H.B.T.I.; Prof. S.K. Awasthi, Head, Dept. of Chemical Engg.; Prof. A.K. Srivastava, Head, Dept. of Chemistry; Prof. S.J. Pande, Head, Dept. of Mechanical Engg.; Dr. Ashok Kumar, Head and Dr. A.K. Singh, Dept. of Physics; Dr. Pramod Kumar, Dr. R.K. Trivedi and Dr. V.K. Tyagi, Dept. of Oil and Paint Technology; Dr. G.P. Bagaria and Dr. (Mrs.) T. Gupta, Head, Dept. of Electronics; Dr. S.K. Mandal, Dept. of Bio-chemical Engg., for their inspiration towards this endeavour.

My thanks are also due to my department faculty members Dr. (Mrs.) B. Nigam, Mr. K.S. Singh and Mrs. Nidhi G. Kapoor and Ph.D. Scholar Ms. Kavita Srivastava, who have helped me in compiling and editing this book.

I am extremely thankful to all contributors who have taken keen interest and pains to write and contribute research articles for inclusion in this book.

I convey my high gratitude to Mr. Ashok Kumar Mittal of Concept Publishing Company, New Delhi for publication of this book.

At the end, I am thankful to Mr. Sanjay Mishra for his skillful typing and processing works for this book.

K.M. Mohapatra

Contents

Section II
A Haromony Between 'Materialism' and 'Spiritualism' through an Appropriate Technological Revolution

Section III
Human Values and Environment

Section IV
Impact of Information and Computer Technology on Human Values

List of Contributors

S.K. Awasthi, Professor and Head, Department of Chemical Engg., H.B.T.I., Kanpur, U.P.

A. Balasubramanian, Assistant Registrar, Bharathidasan University, Ponnager, Trichy, Tamil Nadu.

Sanjeev Batra, Scholar, Department of Computer Engg., H.B.T.I., Kanpur, U.P.

Ira Das, Reader (Psychology), Department of Social Sciences, DEI, Dayalbagh, Agra, U.P.

Sahab Das, Training and Placement Officer and Faculty of Engg., DEI, Dayalbagh, Agra, U.P.

K.K. Ghosh, Professor and Head (Electrical Engg.), H.B.T.I., Kanpur, U.P.

V.K. Jain, Director and Professor (Computer Engg.), H.B.T.I., Kanpur, U.P.

Sudhira Chandra Jena, Lecturer, P.G. Department of Political Science, F.M. College, Balasore, Orissa.

K. Krishna Priya, Scholar, Department of Computer Engg., JNTU College of Engg., Anantpur, Andhra Pradesh.

Pradeep Kumar, Lecturer, Department of Civil Engg., H.B.T.I., Kanpur, U.P.

Pramod Kumar, Lecturer (Paint Technology), Department of Oil and Paint Technology, H.B.T.I., Kanpur, U.P.

C.M. Mishra, Lecturer, Department of Computer Science, Institute of Basic Sciences (Dr. B.R. Ambedkar University), Khandari, Agra, U.P.

K.M. Mohapatra, Assistant Professor, Department of Humanities and Social Sciences, H.B.T.I., Kanpur, U.P.

Gurpreet Nagi, Research Associate, Department of Family Resource Management, Punjab Agricultural University, Ludhiana, Punjab.

Ajay S. Patil, Lecturer, Department of Computer Science, North Maharashtra University, Jalgaon, Maharashtra.

Geetanjali S. Patil (Mrs.), Lecturer, Department of Education, Shivaji University, Kolhapur, Maharashtra.

S. Padmasani Kannan (Mrs.), Principal, M.A.M. College of Catering and Hotel Management, Chennai, Tamil Nadu.

I. Ramachandra Reddy, Principal and Professor (Civil Engg.) Chaitanya Bharathi Institute of Technology, Gandipet, Hyderabad, Andhra Pradesh.

Binayak Rath, Professor (Economics), Department of Humanities and Social Sciences, IIT, Kanpur, U.P.

Raka Saran, (Mrs.) Professor (Sociology), Department of Humanities and Social Sciences, IIT, Kanpur, U.P.

V.K. Saraswat, Lecturer, Department of Computer Science, Institute of Basic Sciences (Dr. B.R. Ambedkar University), Khandari, Agra, U.P.

N.R. Shapre, Department of Education, Shivaji University, Kolhapur, Maharashtra.

Shraddha Shukla (Mrs.), Lecturer, Department of Teacher Education, D.W. Training College, Kanpur, U.P.

A.K. Singh, Lecturer, Department of Physics, H.B.T.I., Kanpur, U.P.

Jitendra Kumar Singh, Research Scholar, Department of Civil Engg., H.B.T.I., Kanpur, U.P.

Manu Pratap Singh, Lecturer, Department of Computer Science, Institute of Basic Sciences (Dr. B.R. Ambedkar University), Khandari, Agra, U.P.

Deepak Srivastava, Lecturer, Department of Plastic Technology, H.B.T.I., Kanpur, U.P.

M. Subbarayudu, Professor (Electronics), Department of ECE, JNTU College of Engg., Anantpur, Andhra Pradesh.

M.K. Dhillon (Mrs.), Professor and Head, Department of Family Resource Management, Punjab Agricultural University, Ludhiana, Punjab.

G. Vidyanath, Faculty Member, School of Management Studies, Chaitanya Bharathi Institute of Technology, Gandipet, Hyderabad, Andhra Pradesh.

B. Vijaya Mary, Scholar (Electronics and Communication Engg.), JNTU College of Engg., Anantpur, Andhra Pradesh.

M.M. Uplane (Mrs.), Department of Education, Shivaji University, Kolhapur, Maharashtra.

Introduction

K.M. Mohapatra

I

For the last few years, 'sustainable development' has become a matter of great concern among the scientists. 'Protection of human being and his environment' from the adversities of industrialisation and technological expansion has been the slogan all over the world. There is fear that if the adversities of industrialisation are not abated since now, the entire process of development may be jolted one day. A world wide devastation may take place. In order to save the human from that menace, the prudent groups have started thinking of the possibility of environment-friendly industrialisation and eco-friendly technological inventions as to bring back the developmental process much more closed to the nature. An environment-friendly technological development could cause conditions for the sustainment of the entire development process.

The human always tries his best to lead a prosperous and comfortable living through a process of development. But, the development is to face the challenges of the natural constraints. In order to get rid of the natural constraints and adversities, since time immemorial, the human has been keeping himself busy in discovering new things and inventing new techniques in various fields. Through that process, he expands his scope of knowledge about the facet of the nature. The ultimate aim of all exercises of the human is to maximise his pleasure and happiness. One may seek more pleasure from comfortable living or another may craze for knowledge for more happiness in life. A saint, following spiritualistic paths, can fulfil his desire for salvation of life from which he gets heavenly pleasure. On the other hand, a common man believing happiness in worldly things tries his best to accumulate them for fulfilment of material desires. In both instances, the ultimate objective of a human is to attain optimum pleasure and minimum pain. In all cases, more and more satisfaction is the ultimate end. For the sake of achieving more pleasure, the people start competition among themselves. Every one tries his best to be superior to others; say, either in possessing wealth or in the field of acquiring knowledge. This competitive tendency in human creates endless desires in him. A person, who has plenty of wealth to meet his desires, gets into more comfortable living and once plunging in paucity of resources passes through a miserable living. From ones perception, today's scientific inventions and discoveries have no less contribution towards the human competition for more pleasure. Such competitive tendency in human makes him highly selfish, myopic and self-centred. When one does something for his own-interest, he rarely bothers about the adverse reflection of his deeds on others. For example, when a scooterist drives away on a road, he rarely cares about his scooter's smoke suffocating the pedestrians; when a nation applies its nuclear weapons against its enemies in a war, it rarely bothers about its adversity on the environment; and so on. In present scenario of development, the moral values in human are gradually missing.

It is quite certain that technological breakthrough and advancement are warranted in order to defiantly face the challenges of population explosion and changing human requirements. Natural resources, which were to be explored and brought to human use with the help of technology, are some renewable and some other non-renewable. The renewable resources have optimal limits to be exploited and, again, they require minimal time limits for renewability, corresponding to a certain technological level. Any technological interference with these resources violating extreme limits of exploitation and renewability for the sake of overexploitation, would definitely cause adversities on the environment as well as on the living beings. Overexploitation of common property resources like land, forests, rivers, lakes, fisheries, seas, etc, which has been made possible due to technological inventions, can be taken for citations. Non-renewable resources like minerals are overexploited because of excessive pressure of massive industrialisation. Imbalanced industrialisation and urbanisation, along with increasing influence of consumerism all over, have led both renewable and non-renewable resources to be overexploited beyond limits by the human. Technological inventions in different fields of knowledge have made the human over-enthusiastic for possessing wealth and power. Moral and ethical values, which rest at higher level of consciousness and rationality in human, have been deteriorating. That has made him highly selfish, myopic and self-centred. Owing to that, the sustainable development and stability of the social and the natural orders have become doubtful.

By 'human values' we mean to human principles or standards and human judgement of what is valuable or important in life. Human values are the reflection of good qualities in human thoughts and actions. These emerge from inner parts of a being and base on his higher level of rationality, self-realisation and enlightenment. Human values incorporate all virtues and dissipate vices in him. These also refer to 'moral' or 'ethical' values in human, which are accepted by the society at time as required standards that ought to be maintained by the human for the safeguard of the social and natural orders and for keeping family and professional life happy. A society can attain optimum welfare if its members are highly disciplined with a higher level of rationality and moral values, even though the society possessing a lower level of growth in physical entities. Perhaps, the main objectives of religions, rituals and customs are to safeguard human values, and to direct the mankind towards spiritualism for self-enlightenment and self-realisation through which the human can develop virtues and eliminate vices in him. From these angles, religion and spiritualism have positive points for development. On the other hand, 'materialism' creates a force in human thoughts which makes him highly inclined to outer objects and temporal pleasures. Selfishness and self-centredness are resulted in human due to unwarranted impact of materialism. These elements may cause demotion of human values and rise of human vices. Today's system of education and discovery of science and technology are believed to be responsible for leading the human being to the state of undesired dominance of materialism over spiritualism, and to the state of dominance of vices over virtues in human.

No doubt, technological breakthrough in many fields has significantly contributed to the physical development of the society and facilitated very comfortable living to the human. But, at the same time, it has made the human being more dependent on mechanical power. It has changed the human thinking processes excessively towards materialism under which influence the human is becoming selfish, myopic and assertive. A possession of physical things has become the main goal of a human. For acquiring power and wealth, in many instances, a common human does not hesitate to commit crimes and corruptions. The all sorts of virtues in a human are shadowed by his vices. In his mind, the noble desires are subjugated by the evil desires. The philanthropic thoughts in him are gradually disappearing. In this context, many doubts are arisen about—when the mentality of the people is changing towards excessive materialism and consumerism, can they think of about welfare of the society as a whole? Can one think of benefit of another? Will they think about the protection of environment from the adversity of industrialisation? and so on.

Focusing on Indian society, if the past structure is compared to the present one, we could mark a radical change in many aspects. As the Indian society is heading towards higher level of industrialisation and unbanisation, the human relations are changing very rapidly. The traditional joint family system has collapsed. The joint families have splitted up into nucleus families. The human relations between husband and wife, between parents and children, between brothers and sisters, and between teachers and students have shown the indication towards new directions. The traditional human value system is at the verge of disappearance. Such changes are very fast among the Indian youngsters. Such changes in human relations in Indian society are mostly due to the influence of the western materialistic socio-culture. It is contextual to mention that today's development in networking of global information system through computer technology has no less contribution to such changes among Indian youngsters. No doubt, information technology and computers provide immense facilities to the development in the fields of agriculture, trade and business, education, medical science, library science, etc. but, at the same time, these cause adversities, particularly on the children's morality and psychology, through the process of making them easy access to certain immoral and anti-social scenes such as pornography, nudity, e-crime, etc. Consequently, in many instances, marriage and sex related crimes are reported of being increased. Perhaps, towards the early beginning of the next millennium, India will be going to face the same human relation problems what the western countries do have today.

It is certain that such changes in human as well as in social relations could not be stopped. Instead, it would not be impossible on our part to direct such changes towards a noble direction—a situation of harmony between materialism and spiritualism—balance between physical and non-physical development. For sustaining developmental process for a long time, the non-physical aspects such as human and social values are to be equally emphasised as is being done in the physical aspects of the development.

Since the science and technology has caused the above changes in human thoughts and human relations, we have a strong belief that the scientists can direct the above changes towards a noble horizon with the help of their inventions and discoveries.

II

This book encompasses discussions on three broad aspects: (i) impact of technological progress on the socio-economic conditions and human value system, (ii) technological progress and environmental problems and their impacts on the quality of human living, and (iii) suggestive measures – a kind of scientific and technological revolution for establishing harmony between 'materialism' and 'spiritualism'. In total, four sections are made in order to incorporate the above discussions in a systematic manner. A brief note of each section is given below.

Section I is entitled "Technological Progress and Quality of Life". It consists of six essays. Contributors to this section are – Prof. Binayak Rath, Prof. Raka Sharan, Prof. K.K. Ghosh, Dr. Pramod Kumar with Dr. Deepak Srivastava, Mr. N.R. Shapre with Mr. M.M. Uplane and Mr. Pradeep Kumar with Mr. Jitendra Kumar Singh.

Prof. Rath inquires into how technological advancement has become a threat to human value system, how technology is a means for the structural changes of the socio-cultural, economic and political organisations and how these changes deviate from the human values and affect quality of human life.

Mr. Shapre and Mr. Uplane have looked into the positive contributions of science and technology to the improved quality of human living. For making human life more beautiful and dignified, moral values ought to be attached to the scientific inventions.

Mr. Pradeep Kumar and Mr. Singh stress on the socio-economic disparities and degradation of human value system owing to technological progress.

Prof. Sharan attempts to interlink the engineering product design and social values. She discusses different value dimensions of engineering design of a product, and how social values influence the mental processes of the human and, again, how the engineering design is dependent upon the mental processes.

Dr. Pramod Kumar and Dr. Srivastava discuss relationships between human values and quality of life as well as between technological progress and unhealthy practices that go against human and social values. Factors influencing human values are also explained by them.

Prof. Ghosh explains five domains of human values— truth, righteous conduct, peace, love and non-violence, with picture presentation. He also focuses on how technological inventions and technology transfer are collated to the above domains of human values.

Section II is "A Harmony between 'Materialism' and 'Spiritualism' through An Appropriate Technological Revolution". It has six essays. Contributors to this section are —Dr. K.M. Mohapatra and Prof. V.K. Jain, Dr. G. Vidyanath with Prof. I. Ramachandra Reddy, Geetanjali S. Patil, Prof. S.K. Awasthi with Dr. A.K. Singh, Dr. S. Padmasani Kannan and Dr. Sahab Das with Ira Das.

Dr. Mohapatra and Prof. Jain, with the help of a logistic model, describe how sustainable development and maximisation of social welfare are achieved through conjucting Social Mental Force (SMF) and Social Object Force (SOF). How can the technological and scientific transformation bring about the above conjuction? They attach metaphysical perceptions to the sustainable development.

Dr. Vidyanath and Prof. Reddy focus their attention on the various socio-economic adversities of the technological progress, and owing to that, how the consideration of human value system is neglected. They also stress on the possibility of interlinkage of scientific and technological progress and development of spiritualism.

Dr. (Mrs.) Geetanjali Patil attempts to connect scientific inventions to spiritualism and quality of life. She explains how erosion of human values will be stopped.

Prof. Awasthi and Dr. Singh illustrate the adversities of scientific discoveries on the human moral values with reference to Indian societies. They examine the negative impacts of certain technologies in the fields of mass media, internet and genetic engineering. They also discuss how value based education in traditional lines would be helpful in attaching human values to scientific inventions and their applications.

Dr. Kannan's essay includes discussions of science, technology, materialism and spiritualism. How excessive influence of materialism and consumerism has caused deterioration of ethical values among Indians and how ethical considerations, cultural affinities, technological progress and human life are interlinked.

Dr. Das and Ira Das discuss technological awareness, value judgement of a technology, mitigation of attainments and values, creative visualisation of technology through inner stability, concentration and balance between spiritualism and 'materialism'.

Section III is entitled "Human Values and Environment". It consists of five essays. Contributors are Dr. M.K. Dhillon with Gurpreet Negi, Dr. Sudhira Chandra Jena, Dr. Shraddha Shukla, A. Balasubramanian and Dr. K.M. Mohapatra.

Dr. Dhillon and Negi's essay on 'Human values and environment' is based on empirical study conducted by them. They focus on the issues — how noise pollution in Ludhiana, Punjab, is largely attributable to massive use of household equipment/appliances which are the contributions of modern technology, and how the loss of human values both at the stages of inventions and applications of these things are the causes.

Dr. Jena finds relationship between man-nature and human values. He cites examples – how man and nature were interacting in congenial manner, and how industrial revolution had changed this interaction. He stresses on the system of education to man, which can restore values in him so as to establish cordial interaction between the nature and the man.

Dr. Shukla discusses duality in man's nature and value system *vis-à-vis* environment.

Balasubramanian attempts to interlink economy, environment and human values by citing and quoting versions of great personalities.

Dr. Mohapatra in his essay, "Environmental pollution attributable to technology transfer to immoral persons: experience from primary sector", highlights on – how did technological progress in agriculture, mining, quarrying and fishing lead to overexploitation of natural resources, and consequently, to environmental pollution and ecological imbalance? How human value consideration is missed in technological and scientific applications with special reference to transgenic crop technology, which is one of the causes of environmental degradation. How is technology transfer to unscrupulous and immoral persons responsible for the above problems? He suggests that the technological inventions and transfer should be harmonized with human values.

Section IV is "Impact of Information and Computer Technology on Human Values". It contains five essays. Contributors are Prof. V.K. Jain, B. Vijaya Mary with K. Krishna Priya and Prof. M. Subbarayudu, Sanjeev Batra, Manu Pratap Singh with C.M. Mishra and V.K. Saraswat and A.S. Patil.

Prof. Jain highlights both advantages and disadvantages of information technology with reference to agricultural and service sectors, business world and education system. He also examines the role of information society in the above regard, and suggests how the negative impacts of IT can be minimized by imbibing moral and spiritual values in the users.

Vijaya Mary, *et al*. discuss information and communication revolution, and analyse how this has been pivotal factor for the global economic development. They argue in favour of a moral value-based technological revolution, particularly in IT areas.

Batra, in his essay, narrates how IT has threatened human relations and human honesty. He foresees the situations in coming century in which IT will play importantly in the developmental processes, but its negative aspects will be so aggressive that it may thwart the entire process of social order and human relations.

Singh, *et al*. provide a balanced view on the role of IT in the developmental process. They highlight the role of IT in the fields of internet connectivity, distant education, internet-telephone, high-tech medical instrument, digital library, and so on. In negative aspects, they discuss about high-tech cheating, virtual nudity, unemployment, etc.

Patil states about how IT has become helpful in enhancing social awareness in matters of dowry issues, problem of child labour, illiteracy, AIDS, superstitions, etc. How children and teenagers are victimized by pornography on the web site; how women are abused through technical manipulation of the electronic medium. He points out e-crimes. He suggests that IT will have significant positive contribution to social and personal growth of human, if it is used reasonably and effectively.

III

All authors have agreed that the technological breakthrough in various fields of human needs has substantially contributed to the economic growth process. On the other hand, such technological revolution has caused certain negative impacts on the human value system as well as on the environment. Moreover, the trend of these negative impacts has been increasing year after year. This may be mainly attributable to the changes that take place in human attitudes and psychology. 'Materialism' dominates over 'spiritualism' in human thoughts. Massive industrialisation and urbanisation due to technological revolution are the causes of the above changes in human thoughts. Many think that 'peace' and 'happiness' lie only in money and wealth. However, sooner or later, such changes in human thoughts will thwart the human values and social order, and drag the society to a tragic situation in which sustaining development will be difficult. Foreseeing all these consequences, many authors are of the opinion that 'value judgement' must be a fundamental norm to be strictly followed while a technology is developed in the laboratory, while a technology transfer is made, and while users use it for benefits. Nevertheless, the entire education system — curriculum, teachers and teachings — should be modified and designed in such a manner that there will be adequate scope for the students of present and future generation, by which moral and ethical value system can be sufficiently inducted in their minds. So that conception of 'materialism' and 'spiritualism' in them can be balanced.

Since these are the views of many great personalities culled from various branches of engineering, technology, sciences and arts, I hope this book will be a very valuable contribution to the knowledge as well as very useful for the teachers and students pursuing higher studies, especially in technical and scientific lines.

SECTION I

TECHNOLOGICAL PROGRESS AND QUALITY OF LIFE

1

Technological Advancement as a Threat to Human Value System

Binayak Rath

Introduction

Though the neo-classical and modern economists had heralded the role of capital and technology to bring about higher economic development, they have failed to recognize the baneful effects of those technologies. On the other hand, the radical classical economists like Karl Marx and Frederick Engle had argued that the process of technological progress via capital accumulation would be responsible for collapse of the capitalist system. While the neo-Marxists have carried forward the same argument and advocated for structural changes, the structuralists as well as the new environmental economists have severely criticized the role of science and technology in promoting human welfare. Even, the modern economists like Prof. Amartya Sen, and Gunnar Myrdal have expressed their skepticism about the role of technology on the ground that it is devoid of human values. Instead of promoting welfare, it destroys the human value system which is the basic pillar of development of any society. Thus, the issues associated with science and technology have to be critically examined by the scientific community, social scientists and the policy planners.

I have made an attempt in this paper to focus on some those aspects on the basis of theoretical knowledge gained and with the help of my interactions with various public sector undertakings and industries as a consultant. Specifically, my concern on rehabilitation and resettlement (R&R) policies pursued by various industrial organisations and irrigation project authorities has brought new insight into my thought process of our development patterns which are reflected in this paper.

Technology as a Means for Progress of the Society

The neo-classical economists had envisaged a greater role for technology to intiate the process of economic development and thereby to bring improvement in the quality of life. Taking clue from the Harrod-Domar model of growth, Prof. Robert M. Solow (1956) had developed a new endogenous growth model where technological progress is considered as a residual. On the other hand, Prof. Kenneth Arrow (1962) had attempted to render technological progress as an endogenous variable in the growth model based on "learning by doing". Thus, the new growth theory has endogenised both technological progress and human capital formation. In Robert Lucas (1988) analysis, endogenous technological change has a "growth effect" beyond simply the "level effect" of the learning by doing models.

Due to the significant contributions of science and technology in the production process, the world output had increased by more than 9 times in the post-industrial revolution period (1850-1960) and the per capita income expanded by nearly 4 times. Of course, these changes were not uniform across the different countries of the world. Indeed, the changes in the industrial countries stood out a sharp contrast to pre-industrial countries, which were more or less stagnated as elucidated by Ricardo, Malthus and Mill. While in the pre-industrial countries the "power of population" marched almost in line with "power of production" (hence, resulting in stagnation), the changes in the industrial countries stood out in sharp contrast. Contrary to the developments in LDCs, during this period when the population of rich countries nearly trebled, the output increased over 20 times due to the capital deepening process. The per capita output rose by more than 7 times. Thus, the faint noise of their "population explosion" was drowned in the thunder of their "economic explosion" due to the unprecedented expansion of capital and technology.

The same trend has been strenghthened in the recent years. The annual rate of growth of the rich countries in the 1960s and 1970s was more than 5 per cent, with Japan attaining growth rate around 10 per cent. In those economies, the production process has been revolutionised; while the doubling of total goods and services is taking place about every 15 years, the doubling time will shrink in future. Alvin Toffler in *Future Shock* (1970) envisaged that behind those prodigious economic facts lied that great, growling engine of change — technology. He regarded technology as a great engine, a mighty accelerator and knowledge as the fuel.

Another futurologist, Daniel J. Boorstein, is an eloquent defender of technology. In his book, *The Republic of Technology: Reflection on Our Future Community* (1978), he has argued that technological revolutions are irreversible. Technology, which to him transcends political boundaries, language, religion and local tradition, possesses converging powers that can harmonise the culture and human race. The supreme law of his Republic of Technology convergence, the tendency for everything to become more like everything else.

Thus, technological progress has brought many refreshing changes in the world economy in the form of its blessings. It is considered as a means to improve the quality of life by way of industrial development, agricultural development, social and infrastructure development in irrigation, power, education, road and rail network, transport system, sanitation, and safe drinking water provisions, communication network development and by way of promoting defence and offence capabilities of the countries. It also provides a number of consumer durable items for the comfort of the mankind. Even, technology is playing a lead role in the film and television industry as well as in the beauty pageants.

In addition to bringing these transformations in the society, technology is also responsible for introducing many structural changes.

Structural Changes via Technological Progress

Introduction of any new technology into the production process has brought about a number of structural changes in the economic realm, socio-political spheres, bureaucratic administration, cultural and aesthetic behaviour of the society. For instance, India's traditional manufacturing industry suffered a set back when machine-made goods started coming into India from Britain. In competition with the machine industry, India's cottage industry collapsed and India became a predominantly agricultural country, producing only foods. The township broke up workers returned to land owing to the structural changes.

A similar trend was also observed in Europe during the industrial revolution, which brought in a new role for science and technology. The ushering of industrial revolution in Europe too brought a number of structural changes in the field of economics, politics, religion and culture. It had resulted in "deserted village" and "enclosure movements".

In order to gauge those structural changes, various approaches associated with technological advancement are adopted by the social scientists and policy planners. Those approaches are:

1. *Engineering Approach*, with a focus on higher production and productivity, *i.e.*, efficiency measure. It is based on the philosophy that technology can bring about a better world environment. Science and technology can conquer everything on the earth as well as that of the outer space. However, in their zeal to attain higher technical efficiency, the technology managers lose sight of the equity and social justice aspects of development. One best such example can be cited as that the irrigation engineers are generally insensitive to the R&R problems of the dam oustees. Their approach is at best confined to the payment of monetary compensation, which brings a lot of miseries for the project affected persons (PAPs).

2. *Economic Approach,* based on economic parameters like national income or standard of living of the people. The economists argue that with the help of technology, the production process will change rapidly and thereby bring rise in national income of the countries as well as the standard of living of the people. This functional approach of the economists is also suffering from a number of lacuna, which can be avoided by adhering to the human development index (HDI).
3. *Political Approach,* based on political systems and their norms, which will vary along with socio-economic changes and changes in the political and economic institutions. Yet, the political structure will be more responsive to the needs of the people.
4. *Socio-economic Approach,* with a focus on social and human value system that gives rise to a dualistic structure. The application of science and technology will bring about changes in education, healthcare, employment patterns, social institutions and social values, which give rise to dualism.
5. *Environmental Approach,* with a focus on pollution abatement and regeneration of environment, i.e., sustainable development. The environmentalists argue that technology brings misery with it due to loss of their physical, economic, political and developmental control of environment. Science and technology is in conflict with the environment after certain stage. The harmony between technology and environment is lost when the production process based on new technology exceeds the carrying capacity of the environment.
6. *Cultural Approach,* based on traditions and cultural values. Technology will bring a new culture with it, where the traditional culture will be squeezed by the modern culture.

In view of these varying approaches, a number of structural changes have taken place. For instance, the application of science and technology in the modern industrial sector has given rise to organisational dualism, structural dualism and technological dualism in the developing economies like ours. Owing to existence of dualism, the technological gap between the modern sector (capital intensive) and traditional sector (labour intensive) further widens. Moreover, due to distortions in the socio-political spheres the gap, instead of being reduced, is widening over the years. Owing to this dichotomy, the development planners face a new challenge, *i.e.*, how to improve the quality of policy-making? How can the strategy and tactics improve? How can better policies be devised and the process of policy-making be made more effective?

Baneful Effects of Technology

The technological progress via industrialisation, which initially promised refreshing optimism, has brought many untold miseries for mankind. Along with myriad technological advances in the fields of production processes, telecommunications, information technology and infrastructure, the economic system has become more brutal and inhuman due to the ecological disaster and pollution emanating from technological progress. In this respect, Daniel J. Boorstein, one of the ardent supporter of technology, has identified the following problems associated with it:

- Technology is a way of multiplying the unnecessary
- Technology insulates and isolates, *i.e.*, while technology seems to bring us together, it does so only by making new ways of separating us from one another; and
- Technology uproots us and separates us from our own special time and place.

Thus, many argue that with this much-eroded physical and socio-economic environment of today we are going to enter the new millennium with the possibility of a global crisis of unprecedented magnitude.

In spite of the positive effects of technology, as mentioned in the preceding section, during 1960s and 1970s, there was a growing criticism regarding the progress of capital/technology deepening process of development. People became skeptical about the trend of development due to rapid environmental degradation, which was closely associated with the process of industrialisation, urbanisation, infrastructure development and extensive and intensive agricultural operations. There was rapid depletion of natural resources, the traditional sources of energy and raw materials. There was disruption of natural resources, the traditional sources of energy and raw materials. The disruption of natural ecological balance, destruction of economic ends of various animal and plant species, the negative genetic consequences of industrialisation and other pollutants posed a serious threat to the environment. To add to it, the technological changes brought a throwaway culture, which also led to significant pollution and the problem of spillover costs. It was argued that man's attempt to conquer the nature through technological progress would threaten to destroy all life on the earth. In view of these ensuing problems, Frederick Engels had warned:

> "Let us not, however, flatter ourselves over much on account of our human victories over the nature. For in each such victory the nature takes its revenge on us. Each victory, it is true, in the first place brings about the results we expected, but in the second and third places, it has quite different, unforeseen effects which only too often cancel the first".

These forewarnings of Lavels have been substantiated by the recent natural calamities in different parts of the globe. One such immediate example is the devastation and casualties caused by the killer cyclone in Orissa during October 29-31, 1999.

To add to it, the growing disenchantment with neo-classical economic growth models and the anti-growth debate initiated in the 1970s led to a considerable discussion on impact of technology on the environment at various international forums. Many economists and social scientists started critical assessment of the development processes and expressed their concern about the environmental dimensions of these processes.

To start with, Kenneth. E. Boulding (1970) in his book *A Primer on Social Dynamics: History as Dialectics and Development*, initiated a new dialogue on the dynamics of the development process where he exhibited the role of ecological system and its depletion due to the new process of development.

In the same vein, Alvin Toffler (1970) in his book *Future Shock* talked of a "Taming Technology Concept" and predicted "In our Haste to Milk Technology for immediate economic advantages we have turned our Environment into a Physical and Social Tinder Box".

Similarly, the authors of *The Limit to Growth* published by the "Club of Rome" in 1972 had focused that in the wake of technological advancement and the consequent industrialisation and urbanisation, there is a need to bring balance between natural resources, its ecology and environment. With the help of "Project Predicament of Mankind", the authors showed the complexity of interconnected problems of technology, environmental degradation, haphazard industrialisation, uncontrolled urbanisation, poverty, inflation, etc. As a drastic alternative to the growth models of development, they had proposed zero growth concept. In its subsequent publication entitled *Reshaping the International Order* (1978), the club had further developed the following propositions:

(a) that the unprecedented scale of human interference with nature and ecological balances via technological progress might prove disastrous to all; and
(b) our life-support systems are under unprecedented attacks from the combined effects of urbanisation, industrialisation, agriculture and our daily life styles.

Maurice Strong (1974) in his book *An Inventory of Hope — The Case for Optimism*, has advocated a comprehensive approach. Among the steps suggested for the survival of mankind, he has focused on a new approach to social decision-making, organisation and re-orientation of science and technology, a new approach to growth, and a revolution in values and behaviour.

Participating in this growth debate, E.J. Mishan (1977) coined the "Third Dismal Theorem", where he has envisaged: "The more Science, Technology and GNP growth, the more Nasty, Brutish, Vile and Precarious becomes Human existence"

Herman Kahn (1979), a pioneer and leader in the fields of public policy analysis and future studies, in his book *World Economic Development: 1979 and Beyond* has also predicted that we natural, social, political and cultural forces are likely to slow the growth of population and production (anti-growth argument) long before the world encounters any fundamentally unmanageable problems of environmental pollution. Kahn was sharply critical about economic growth and then advanced the concept of Social Limit to Growth. He further professed that:

- We are in the midst of great transition;
- Human society changing at an accelerating pace;
- The future will not be problem free; and
- We do not rule out the possibility of an overwhelming catastrophe.

Human Values as Embeded with Technological Progress

Although the classical economists like T. R. Malthus (1798) and John Stuart Mill (1848) had focused on the human values and morality for higher economic development, they could not establish the link between technology and human values. Indeed, the classical economists failed to foresee the extent and persistence of technological revolution that swept through the developed part of the world in the later part of 18th century and during 19th century. It is the neo-classical economists who stressed the role of technology. They argued that technological progress was more than sufficient to off-set the dismal consequences emanating from diminishing returns and population growth. To them, the thunders of population growth will be swayed away by the technological advancement.

But the philosophy that technological progress could bring higher economic development, as propounded by the neo-classical economists, was challenged by a number of economists. In this respect Throstein Veblen occupies a leading position in criticising the theories and propositions of neo-classical economists. To Veblen, the neo-classical school was excessively static and dedutive, and neglected the element of change in economic life. Through his scholarly incursion into philosophy, he focused on human values, which is best reflected in his piece of work *Theory of Leisure Class: An Economic Study of the Evolution of Institutions* (1899).

Mrs. Joan Robinson in her book *Economic Philosophy* (1962) has also provided a succinct critique of neo-classical economics and the use of metaphysical and ideological propositions in economic theory. She expresses what is known as the relativist view of economic theory — that economic ideas cannot be divorced from the society in which they originate or find application. Hence, human values ought to be included in the writings and works of economists and policy planners.

On the other hand, one of the "holistic thinkers" of the modern Green Movement, E.F. Schumacher in his classic *Small is Beautiful: A Study of Economics as if People Mattered* (1973) has examined the economic structure of the Western World in a revolutionary way. He maintains that one of the most fateful errors of the modern age is the belief that the problem of production has been solved by application of technology. There is an illusion of unlimited powers, nourished by astonishing scientific and technological achievements. He further maintains that man's current pursuit of profit and progress through capital and technology, which promote giant organisations and increased specialisation, has in fact resulted in gross economic inefficiency, environmental hazards, inhumane working conditions and loss of human values. By challenging the propositions of the neo-classical economists that the rich countries should pursue 'education for leisure' and the poor countries to adopt the means of 'transfer of technology', he has proposed a system of Intermediate Technology, based on smaller working units, communal ownership, and regional workplaces utilising local labour and resources. It is said that these ideas of Schumacher are heavily drawn from the writings of Mahatma Gandhi, who has stressed on small and appropriate technology based on local resources. Hence, human values are ought to be taken into consideration in designing our economic policies.

In view of these criticisms towards technology-led development, it is argued that better policies, no doubt, depend on better ideas with a focus on human value systems. It is the quality of education rather than quantity which matters the most for attaining the goal of maximum social welfare. The policy formulators should take into consideration the predictions and prescriptions of economists, and assimilate the state-centred forces of the technocrats and bureaucrats as well as society-centred forces of different classes, interest groups, political parties and above all the voters. But as both the society and the state-centred forces are highly influenced by the human value systems, it is put forth by the liberals that human value will play lead role in the future years to come.

In view of these criticisms, I would like to say that the new growth theory with emphasis on human capital has wider implications for the developing countries. These countries will face the crisis in their value systems. The indegenous value systems will come in conflict with the Western/imported values. This will lead to a dualistic structure that perpetuates the conflict between the two systems. Hence, it is felt that in promoting technology and human capital front, the human value system should be given a higher value with a focus on morality, honesty and integrity.

Concluding Observations

In recent years, international development has undergone a profound transformation in response to tough new realities in the developed and developing economies of the world. At the same time, new windows of opportunities are opening for improving life on our planet. A holistic vision is emerging, one that will place high priority to sustainable development with a greater focus on human values and moral systems. Prof. Sen's concept of sensibility is gaining ground and it will dominate in all discussions of the next millennium. In this new endeavour, it is man's moral values rather than his contributions to technology that will take the front seat and play the lead role. Besides, science and technology must be integrated with human values. Therefore, human values, which have been crushed by the new process of development, ought to be reinstated by the policy planners, technology managers and, above all, by the decision-makers for ensuring a just society in future.

References

Boorstin, Daniel, J. (1978), *The Republic of Technology: Reflections on Our Future Community*, Ambika Publishers, New Delhi.

Cochrane, R. (1985), *Power of the People*, Newnes.

Galbraith, J.K. (1967), *The New Industrial Estate*, H. Hamilton, London.

Grey, Alexander and Thompson, A.E. (1980), *The Development of Economic Doctrine*, Longman Group Limited, London.

Kahn, Herman (1979), *Word Economic Development: 1979 and Beyond*, Morrow Quill, New York.

Rath, Binayak (1999), "Environmental Economics: Issues, Policies, Strategies and Perspectives", the presidential address delivered in the *31st Annual Conference of the Orissa Economic Association*, Talcher College, Talcher, Orissa, February 13-14.

Rath, Binayak (1990), "Environmental Hazards of the Talchar Industrial Complex and their Socio-Economic Impacts in the Brahmani flood-plain", in L.N. Pattanaik, *Environmental Imapcts of Industrial and Mining Activities*, Asian Publishing House, New Delhi.

Rath, Binayak (1997), *"Retrofit Socio-Economic Study of Project Affected Families/Persons on Account of Land Acquisition by the Feroze Gandhi Unchahar Power Project (FGUTPP)"*, Raibarely, Uttar Pradesh, Memeo, I.I.T. Kanpur.

Rath, Binayak (1996), *"EIA Study of the Faridabad Gas based Power Project (FGBPP)"*, NTPC Limited, Faridabad, Haryana, Memeo I.I.T. Kanpur.

Schumacher, E.F. (1973), *Small is Beautiful*, Vintage, London.

Sen, Amartya (1986), *Poverty and Famines: An Essay on Entitlement and Deprivation*, Oxford University Press, New Delhi.

Singh, Virender (1976), *Economics and the Crisis of Ecology*, Oxford University Press, New Delhi.

Toffler, Alvin (1970), *Future Schock*, Pan Books Ltd., London.

Toffler, Alvin (1980), *The Third Wave*, William Morrow Co. Ltd, New York.

2

Technology for Elevating Quality of Life

N.R. Shapre and *M.M. Uplane*

Every living organism is a marval of built-in-technology with man at apex. There is no doubt that the standard of living currently enjoyed by man is significantly higher than what prevailed before industrial revolution. This transformation was possible only due to science and technology with their varied forms. Even though science and technology have bestowed several benefits in opening up new avenues of living and working, they have also created a series of problems, mainly from social, political and economic areas, which lead to degradation of human life.

Is technology responsible for degradation of quality of human life? If so, what components of technology are affecting the quality of life? If we are successful in identifying these components of technology, what measures are to be used to maintain or upgrade the quality of life by using technology.

For answers to the above questions, we must know exact meaning of technology. In a simple meaning, technology is the application of scientific knowledge. How this scientific knowledge emerges? Knowledge is a common heritage of human kind. Knowledge is the only treasure of human kind that can provide a possible remedy to action of the quality of life. Hence, in a broader sense technology means sets of instruments, skills, principles, rules, etc., which are invented from various disciplines of sciences, and usage of such sets to satisfy the needs of a society or a community.

It is clear that technology has its origin from needs of the human being. For example when Watt invented steam engine, he substituted mechanical power for muscle power and then, industrial revolution began. This industrial revolution in Europe, emergence of capitalism and European colonialism...... all these things happened in same duration. This, of course, does not mean that origin of science and technology was only from Europe. However, it is mentioned by Joseph Needam that the Eastern culture from China and India was leading a prosporus life with the help of advanced techniques. Hence, it is necessary to take review of technological progress and its impact on human life.

Table 2.1: Technological inventions for human life

S. No.	*Technological Inventions*	*Impact on Human Life*
1.	Tools and weapons (Neolithic age)	Selected down in one place
2.	Ploughs blades and wheels (Mesopatamian)	Farming and housing and transport
3.	Craftsmanship in designing, weaving and construction (2300 to 1700 B.C.)	Houses, cities, drainage and sewage system
4.	Printing	—
5.	Industrial revolution	Development of locomotives
6.	Manufacture of H_2So_4	Development of chemical industry.
7.	Idea of electric and magnetic field	Modern communication technology and modern day living
8.	Transport technology	Communication with automobile

After the above evolution, new branches of technology had arisen in the fields of molecular engineering, genetic engineering, nuclear science and instrumental technology. We have witnessed spectacular developments in these areas just in couple of decades.

Although each and every technology has made the human life smooth and easy, as many thinkers argue, it has completely neutralized the value system, and also, it is totally unrelated to social and moral responsibility. Is it so?

For clarifying this concept, we should explain the real meaning of human life. Biologically speaking, human being is just an animal occupying the apex of evolution. But, what is this apex? It is a high stage in evolution, high stage in intellect, reason, thinking and act. Human differs from other animals in many ways; the most important difference is the needs of human and the ways for fulfilling the needs.

There are four types of needs of human—physical, intellectual, spiritual and social. For fulfilling these needs, every human selects, understands, discriminates and evaluates for searching the way. In this process, he creates his own environment, especially a social environment. Every human being attempts to create a totality of social environment. Thus the goal of human is the pursuit of an ideal good human life.

For achieving a goal, every human has to use his power and capacity at the highest degree. Here comes the use of technology. We can see that each and every invention has the main aim to increase the human capacity may be of work, *i.e.* muscle, as in machine; may be of logical thinking process as in computers; may be use of time as in communication; and so on.

Can't we say that these inventions have a great impact on quality of human life? The answer is yes; the technology has improved the quality of life.

What is a good life? What are its dimensions? The human life has two dimensions: (i) technological perspective of human life, which emphasises utilisation of tools and techniques for benefit of humankind for his own happiness; and (ii) behavioural perspective in which he refines his needs, and adopts such a life style in which the use of technology is minimum for himself, but maximum for others.

When one relates the technology to quality of life, he considers only the first aspect of human life. But when we consider life, the mystery between matter and mind goes deeper and deeper. Hence, Charles Sherrington, a Noble Prize winner (Physiologist) quoted, "thoughts, feelings, are not amenable to the energy-matter concept. They lie outside the Natural Science. This means there are many things beyond science". Our technology is directed towards the way to reach these things.

We use technology for improving the quality of our life and to some extent, we have succeded also. As a result of technological breakthrough, a nation has to achieve an increase in G.N.P., increase in food crops, milk, etc., decrease in infant/ pregnant deaths, control over some epidemics, self-depending in the areas of food, industries, medicines, weapons, etc. and advancement in communications STD/ISD/VSNL-Networking-Inter and Internet-Global Village.

Certainly, technological development has a crucial role in the above. But who is more responsible for this? Of course, human being. When one uses technology for performing a task, he uses his rational thinking capacity for performing the task with minimum efforts, time and money but with maximum output. Hence, by using technology the human being can find a lot of leisure. How to use this leisure.....a main problem for which the technology is being blamed. There are so many technical devices, you have to use after selection and evaluation.

Technology is a weapon which can be used in both directions just like a knife for covering butter over bread or for murdering some one. For maintaining and also for improving the quality of life what is needed is one's rational thinking capacity, and decision-making capacity and morality before action. These three powers are the real gifts to the human being by which one can select, evaluate and use technology not only for benefit of his own life but also for his followers. Then and then only the technology will become useful and fruitful for his life.

We conclude in the words of Einstein: "The most important human endeavour is the striving for morality in our actions. Our inner balance and even our every existence depends on it. Only morality in our actions can give beauty and dignity to life".

References

Barak, M. (1999), *Enhaced Science and Technology from Theory into Practice in Staff and Educational Development International*, Vol. 3, Aravali Books International.

Gaind, D.N. and Sharms, R.P. (1971), *Educational Theories and Modern Trends*, Ram Prasad & Sons, New Delhi.

Gopinath, K. (1996), *Milestones in Science and Technology*, Navakarnataka Publications, Bangalore.

Habib, S.E. (Ed.) (1999), *Situating History of Science Dialogues with Joseph Needam*, Oxford University Press.

Joshi, Luxmanshastri (Ed.) (1997), Marathi Vishwakosh, Vol. 7 *Maharashtra State Mandal*, Mumbai.

Rao, C.N.R. (1999), "Science and Survival" in *Unversity News*, 37(16), April, 1999, AIU, New Delhi.

Sahastrabuddhe, C. (1999), "Science in 21st Century", *Daily Sakal*, 4th September 1999.

Venkitaramanan, S. (1999), "Dilemmas of Development" in *University News*, 37 (7), February 1999, New Delhi.

3

Impact of Science and Technology on Quality of Life

Pradeep Kumar and *Jitendra Kumar Singh*

Introduction

Man has needs, desires and curiosity. These are driving forces for the development of technology. Need for self-preservation brought the hunting tools and farming techniques. This was the beginning of technology in human life. Science has empowered evil tendencies in man and also discovered tools for poverty alleviation and disease eradication. It has brought instant worldwide communication. Science and technology have provided great momentum to the human society. However, we must find out where is it leading us to? The answer lies in sharpen analysis of the nature of the fundamental driving forces behind technology. We ask, for example, what does a hungry man desire to achieve? Does he eat under the dictates of the hunger or does he eat to get rid of hunger? A man below the poverty line looks at hunger as a risk to survival. It brings worry and agony. He wants to get rid of hunger. A well-to-do man is not oppressed by the risk factor. He is at ease and recognizes the normal function of hunger. He lets himself go along the dictates of this impulse and enjoys food eating. This is where the gap between poor and rich is increasing and drawing a thin line between the quality of a poor and a rich person.

The question of quality of life is inseparably interwoven with that of basic needs. It is applied equally to an individual and to the society. The UNESCO (1997) has defined quality of life as "the satisfaction of an inclusive set of human needs which covers all aspects of living including material satisfaction of vital needs as well as more transcendental aspects of life such as personal development, self-realisation and a healthy ecosystem". Quality of life measurement may be viewed as a matrix of parameters concerning objective conditions of reality alongwith perceived satisfaction-indicators in an hierarchy of needs. In quality environmental need, structure should have the following hierarchy of needs at the individual and community level:

1. *Survival needs*: Such as shelter, clothing, cleanliness, preventive and curative medicine to protect life.
2. *Societal needs*: Promotion of community spirit with respect to protection of environment, developing effective mechanism and enforcing norm of social discipline to keep the environment free from degradation.
3. *Cultural needs*: Provision for personal freedom and privacy, equal opportunity for overall growth.
4. *Welfare needs*: Including measures offering a fair deal to the weak, the disabled, the handicapped and the vulnerable for environmental protection.
5. *Progress needs*: Sharpening of problem anticipation and problem solving capabilities, growth of scientific and technological research and development of human engineering skills.

It is often misunderstood that quality of life and standard of living are the same. But there is explicit discrimination between them. Quality of life covers the bare minimum requirements of the facilities giving fullest satisfaction, whereas standard of living needs more facilities than required and rarely gives satisfaction. There is always a greed to achieve more luxuries.

Basic Human Needs in Twentieth Century

Poverty, social and gender inequity are increasing globally and nationally. According to a World Bank report, 1.2 billion people lived on less than $1 per day in 1987. This number increased to 1.3 billion in 1993. Out of 6 billion of the world population, nearly 1.5 billion will live in severe poverty at the dawn of the new millenium. In addition to energy-protein under-and malnutrition, over 2 billion will suffer from micronutrient deficiencies.

Global per capita water supplies are declining and are now 30 per cent lower than they were 25 years ago. By 2050, as much as 42 per cent of the world population will live in countries with insufficient fresh water stocks to meet the combined needs of agriculture, industry and domestic use.

Contaminated drinking water causes diseases that account for 10 per cent of the total burden of diseases in developing countries. In 1996, about 1.4 billion low income and over 400 million middle income people lacked access to sanitary facilities. At the present rate of progress, over 900 million persons will lack adequate sanitation by the year 2015. In one, out of four major cities surveyed by UN Habitat, less than 10 per cent of households had sewerage connections.

Disparities are also growing in access to technology. For example, 97 per cent of all internet hosts are in developed nations, hence to 16 per cent of the world's population. The rapid expansion of proprietary science covered by intellectual property rights is leading to the emergence of "technological apartheid". The rich-poor economic and technological divide is not only causing inequity at the level of the present generation, but also increasing inter-generational inequity. For example, the affluent economies of the temperate zone are likely to impose severe net costs on the tropical regions because of their excessive consumption of fossil fuels, leading to a large release of green-house gases. Panayotou *et al.* point cut that much of the damage caused by a continuous rise in CO_2 concentrations in the atmosphere will occur in tropical countries, especially Africa and India. These two are predicted to suffer adverse agricultural consequences, possibly severe vector-borne diseases, increased risks of severe tropical storms and vulnerability to rising ocean levels.

Economic and Social Imbalance due to Science and Technology

Loss of rural employment and migration from the country side to the cities cause a fundamental and irreversible shift. It has contributed throughout the world to the destabilisation of rural society and to the growth of vast urban concentrations. An increase in urban slums as a result of loss of rural livelihood presents a grave threat to achieving the goal of ensuring every human being access to basic human needs like safe water, sanitation, balanced diets, healthcare and education. The pathway to meeting basic needs to every human being is poverty eradication.

Today, developing countries face additional handicaps including severe debt and debt servicing burdens, an unfair trade regime where trade is becoming free but not fair. Trade policies should be formulated in such a manner that they will strengthen and not erode the livelihood security of women and men living in poverty. Developing countries should ensure that their import and export policies are based on a livelihood impact analysis.

Emerging Scientific Revolutions: A Positive Approach

Fortunately, as we approach to the new century, we are experiencing three major revolutions in science and technology, which will influence agriculture and industry:

- The gene revolutions providing a molecular understanding of the genetic basis of living organisms, as well as the ability to use this understanding to develop new processes and products of agriculture, industry, environment and for human and animal health.
- The ecotechnology revolution promoting the blending of the best in traditional knowledge and technology

with biotechnology, renewable energy and new materials.

- The information and communication revolution allowing a very rapid growth in systematic assimilation and dissemination of relevant and timely information through low cost electronic networks.

Conclusion

We are ending this century with a huge stockpile of scientific discoveries and technological innovations. This is more than adequate to help all nations to provide every adult human being an opportunity for a healthy and productive life and every newborn child a happy future. Unsustainable life styles and degrading poverty exist everywhere. This is the greatest failure of the developmental pathways and strategies adopted during the century.

The formidable power of science and technology can benefit mankind only if we know how to temper it with humanism. It is the duty of every intellectual to nurture and foster the growth of young men and women researchers capable of initiating and managing changes in goals and strategies in the coming century.

References

Diamond, Jared (1997), *Guns, Germs and Steel: The Fate of Human Societies*, W.W. Norton and Co., New York.

Gyan, Mohan (1998), "Science and Spirituality: Their overlap and exclusive domains", The *22nd Nidhu Bhushan Memorial Lecture, Second India Engg. Conference*, Hyderabad.

Panayotou, *et al.* (1999), *Developing Countries and the Control of Climate Change: Emperical Evidence*, Center for International Development, Harvard University, Cambridge.

Swaminathan, M.S. (1994), "Uncommon opportunities: and agency for peace and equitable development"; Report on International Commission on Peace and Food, London and New York.

Sharan, Raka (1999), "Quality of life: A conceptual framework to understand the human needs"; *Proceedings of Inception Workshop at* H.B.T.I. Kanpur.

4

Engineering Product Design and Social Values

Raka Sharan

Introduction

The heart of technological achievement is design. Design in the creative process in which an integrated combination of concepts, techniques, materials and devices is selected to satisfy a set of requirements. Design is not a random process. It proceeds systematically and depends upon available analytic methods to pinpoint the best of the possible alternative combinations of concepts, techniques, materials and devices. But what is meant by best: the most useful, the most aesthetic, the fastest, the biggest, the smallest, the lightest, the heaviest, the strongest, the safest, the most destructive, the cheapest? When a choice is made among competing alternatives, it is either blind or random or based upon some criteria. Since the criteria against which a design choice is measured arises from values, systematic and analytically created designs cannot exist without values. The values towards which a technological design is directed are those characteristics of the ensuing product that are considered desirable. A criterion is the degree of the valued characteristic, which must be obtained before the product is acceptable. If an electric coffeepot is being designed for the consumer market, a valued dimension would probably be economic production (cost), and the criterion of this value might be Rs. 200. Since criteria are quantitative statements about the amount of a value characteristic that must be incorporated a value, when stated precisely and measurably, needs only an "atleast" statement to become a criterion.

In actual technological designs, it is usually necessary to consider several values at once. Sometimes great difficulties arise in trying to meet simultaneously all the criteria of all relevant value dimensions. One way of attacking the problem is to somehow combine all criteria into a composed criterion. This is not impossible if the value dimensions are fairly straightforward, but many are rather complicated. Some of the more straightforward dimensions can be recognised in the design of the Rs. 200 coffeepot. Besides economy, the design might simultaneously optimize other value dimensions such as weight, size and coffee making time. It is relatively easy to identify these physical characteristics and to state precisely the criterion level for each of them, because criteria can be expressed using fundamental scales of measurement.

The problem increases in difficulty when less precisely measurable values also become important elements of design. For example, suppose it is decided that added value dimensions to which the coffeepot should conform are aesthetic appeal, ease of cleaning and social acceptance. Even these values are roughly measurable, but points along these value dimensions cannot be as precisely defined as was possible for dimensions such as weight and time. The ambiguity increases the opportunity for the engineer to unwittingly influence a design which is his own socially determined preferences. For example, design of an aesthetically pleasing coffeepot will be influenced by which is considered to be attractive in the mind of the buyers coming from different kind of cultural backgrounds.

Do engineers have to concern themselves for such design values? The argument can be made that the engineer is concerned solely with scientific and technical matters. This view seems sensible when the engineer's work optimizing some set of value dimensions that have been specified by someone else like a manager or a customer. The argument can also stand even when the engineer finds he must determine values and criteria himself. In this case, it is said that he does not set values in his role as an engineer. Instead, if he determines values, he does so in a managerial role, and this is true whether managerial prerogatives have been delegated to him deliberately or by default. He may also make choices of values for design, not as an engineer, but in the role of a humanitarian. This is illustrated by the engineer who decided to design an expensive safety feature into a piece of industrial equipment because of personal conviction about safety requirements.

Product Design and Social Values

Design cannot be tied to social value by simply saying that the setting of design values is an engineering task. Whether this is true or false boils down to a question of the definition of engineering and will be as arbitrary as that definition. Although the question of who should or does set values arises often, it tends to lead to hopeless argument and, for our purposes, it does not really make any difference. To show the inevitable link between technology and social values, it is sufficient to show that social value influences (determines the course of) technological design. That can be true regardless of who sets the values towards which the engineer works.

There are two distinct ways for social values to influence the outcome of design endeavours. First, the requirements guiding the design may be derived directly from social values. This fairly straightforward point can be illustrated by consumer products designed for the market. An example is the new car of the Agarwal (family) with its shiny chrome, flashy tail-fines, and an engine with horsepower to spare. It was deliberately painted canary yellow and given plush matching Agarwal's social values; the useless horsepower was added so Mr. Agarwal could not feel one-up on Mr. Bansal. Since it is easy for a rich businessman to own a car, the car itself is not sufficient to carry prestige and status value. Instead, extras, especially ostentatious ones, are added and advertised. In short, automobiles are designed in part to satisfy prestige and status values; or, to put it in different words, the engineering design is strongly influenced by social values.

The second way in which social values influence design is

considerably more subtle than the first. It arises from the fact that social values are reflected in the behaviour of the individual. For example, the behaviour of American men who always seem to be hurrying is not surprising in a society where speed and efficiency are highly valued. The values of the society where we are raised are internalized through socialisation and become our individual, personal values. The individual's own values, in turn, affect his daily behaviour often without his awareness.

The degree to which personal values creep into the design process depends upon how clearly and completely requirements are stated. If requirements are stated ambiguously, there is more room for the engineer's personal beliefs to operate. The requirement that a product be "aesthetically pleasing" leaves much room for individual interpretation, because it is hard to get agreement on what is meant by aesthetic. Similarly, the requirement to build a "safe" machine will yield different safety features depending upon the designer's interpretation of what is safe and upon what compromises are made with other values. When requirements are stated unambigously, but not in complete details, the engineer by default may have to fill in the gaps himself. In all these cases, the engineer makes choices arising from his own value system. It is noteworthy that the activity called value engineering arises in part because of engineers who design more sophisticated products than are needed. Value engineers in big companies like General Electric or Philips have the job of examining products and asking the engineers, "Is that wrinkle really necessary to do the job for which the product is designed"? In effect, their job is to keep engineers from letting their personal values overly influence the products they design.

The Effect of Value upon Higher Mental Processes

Product-design requires creative thought and making judgement about alternative solutions to design problems; therefore, if such thinking is influenced by values (attitudes, beliefs), then the ensuing design will also be influenced by values. Much psychological literature is available containing evidence on the influence of personal preferences upon higher mental faculties. Technologists, like other men, simply cannot avoid the influence of social values upon their thinking. Demonstrations exist of the effects of values, as expressed in attitudes and beliefs, upon the most basic mental processes: thinking, memory and perception.

Social values influence thinking in even relatively simple matters like logical syllogisms. Several studies have dealt with the effects of psychological variables upon logical reasoning. In one such study college students were asking to solve a series of syllogisms in which the terms had emotional potential for prejudiced people. After correcting for differences in reasoning ability among subjects, there were still distortions in logic due to the students' social prejudices. For example, high caste students did better than the SC/STs. Further examples of the influence of values upon mental processes are found among experiments with the basic processes of learning the retention. Levin and Murphy have carried out an interesting experiment on learning and forgetting of controversial material. Students tended to learn more rapidly and to forget less rapidly material with which they agreed. The effect of social values upon mental processes has been repeatedly demonstrated with simple perceptual tasks indicating a basic influence upon one of the most fundamental concomitants of reason, visual perception. In one experiment by Bruner and Goodman, children were asked to adjust a circle of light to make it equal to a neutral, gray disk and later to each of several coins. Poor children overestimated the size of coins considerably more than wealthy children, indicating a subjective need for a valued object can influence perception.

Engineering design is dependent upon basic mental processes. These processes are influenced by social values, often without awareness.

Conclusion

Now-a-days the engineers occupy important positions in the area of social production. They are given the post of decision-makers or advisors. Since the end of World War II, and more particularly since the intensification of the cold war, the requirement for engineers and scientists in public service has become increasingly recognised. The Ministry of Science and Technology was established in India to provide "high level formulation of research and development policy". The Advanced Research Projects Agencies were established to sponsor long-range reaserch-projects.

These developments are only examples of the evident interest of the government in science and technology and of the growing influence of scientists and engineers upon the processes and decisions of the government. Efforts to bring scientists and engineers more intimately into the process of governmental decision-making represent significant social trend. In this environment, the view that an engineer is an engineer and a politician a politician seems somewhat obsolete. Social values have been wed to technology as never before, especially in the case of product-designs.

In the history of man, combining technology with values is a relatively recent occurrence, at least in the degree with which it is happening. The engineer is in a position where he must make judgments that flow in part from his technological skill and in part from his social values. Increasingly, technologists find themselves in the predicament of the physician who is forced to make value judgements about human life because of the role in which his technical skill has cast him. It is impossible for a sane man to so split his personality that his role as citizen is completely divorced from his role as an engineer. Since the two roles reside in the same body, they inevitably get merged. Engineers cannot escape the mantle of responsibility merely by stating that their field is technology and nothing more. Politicians are expected to make judgements of international significance, which depend upon an understanding of technical matters. Such judgements can be made more intelligently if they are made by men having both political and technical training. The engineers of today find themselves immersed more and more in public service, more and more at the right hand of those making momentous decisions, and thus involved more in inducing social change. In this environment, does a curriculum top-heavy in scientific and technical subjects adequately prepare the engineering student for his future role in society? The answer is 'no'. Hence, it is very essential that engineers must be taught, along with scientific and technical subjects, something which can make him appreciate the 'social values'.

References

Vernon, Raymond (1985), *The Product Life Cycle Hypothesis in a New Internationl Environment*, Wortzel, H.V. and Wortzel, L.H. editors, Strategic Management of Multinational Corporations: The Essentials, New York: John Wiiey & Sons.

Allison, Graham T. (1971), *The Essence of Decision: Explaining the Cubon Missile Crisis*, Boston: Brown and Company.

Kelman, H.C. (1958), *Compliance, Identification, and Internalization: Three Processes of Attitude Changes*, Conflict Resolution, II.

Raia, Anthony P. (1974), *Management by Objectives*, Glenview, III: Scott, Foresman.

Likert, Rensis (1961), *New Patterns of Management*, New York: McGraw-Hill.

5

Influence of Technological Progress on Human Values

Past, Present and Future

Pramod Kumar and *Deepak Srivastava*

Introduction

Indeed, it is a matter of great satisfaction that the world is progressing technologically very fast in various fields of science. Every next moment, the latest technology is threatened to be obsolete. All industrial concerns and scientists are putting in lot of efforts on day-to-day basis to update their technology to cope with such threats, failing which their survival is bound to have a question mark. If one is not well-informed and well-equipped today about the latest trends and developments in the areas of one's concern, one is likely to be phased out of business by one's business rival. Steady improvement in the quality of the product according to the requirement of the hour, and the cost reduction are the two important driving forces for the progress of sustainable technology and the business in turn. Obviously, the environmental considerations are also to be kept on forefront of considerations, in view of the stringent government regulations for environmental protection. In the time of such a cut-throat competition, pure technological competition has proved to be totally inadequate today for the survival of business. It has almost become an unwritten rule as if one wants to beat one's professional rival purely by having an advanced technology, it is said to be a fool's proposition.

Under these circumstances, the budding engineers and technologists are bound to confuse as to which route to go about. Should they go for the development of technology themselves by spending energy and time, or they should look for a short cut for their sales promotion by following nasty ways for the sole purpose of earning highest order of profits to lead a so-called "good life"?

Quality of Life and Human Values

It is really very unfortunate that the quality of life today is assessed mainly by physical/material things that one possesses. As a consequence, people have stopped thinking almost completely about their basic responsibilities to the society, and the people have totally overlooked their social commitments, and ignored the values of human life. This has created a very pitiable scenario in the present time. You can very easily come across small children boasting like "my car is bigger than that of yours, and mine is air conditioned". Does this not reflect upon the thinking and ideology of their parents indicating about their strong temptation for material things? As a result of this thinking, everyone feels unhappy and simply blames one's neighbours for creating such an environment. We agree that this was there in the past also, but the problem has grown to an intolerably acute level at present, and if the same continues in future, anybody and everybody can very well assess the resultant. Undoubtedly, there is a huge degree of erosion on the concerns for unkeeping the human values, and in the days to come, as can be easily speculated, this is going to be further worsened in this respect.

Here is our humble effort as technologists to visualise as to what is expected of us for the society when the society appears to be standing on the crossroads with the viewpoint of technological progress *versus* human values. We have also to examine whether or not, if yes, to what degree the technological progress is responsible for the erosion of human values of the modern society. Before giving an insight into what we should do at present for upkeeping the human values, let us try to examine critically as to what we understand about human values universally.

In our opinion, the important aspects of human values are the morality, ethics, mutual co-operation, commitment for human welfare and the honesty for everything that you do or think. Let us not confuse here between human values and social values, as the social values are governed by environmental/ climatic conditions and generally vary from place-to-place, time-to-time and community-to community. One particular society may design such a set of social norms as may deem fit for itself at that specific time, and there is every likelihood that the same may be treated as totally unacceptable and heinous for a different society, and also for the same society during a different period of time. On the other hand, every society on the earth, with no exception, has to upkeep human values by exercising mutual co-operation and honesty in deeds, for everyone's welfare. Human values are not society or place-specific. That is the reason why roots of success of the most advanced business houses and technological giants across the world lie in their team work. This may, however, be true, as they say, that they are bound to adopt filthy tactics for competing their rivals in business, and also for the advancement of technology they are interested in. In this materialistic age they, in fact, forget that they must stick to safeguarding the human values even at the cost of some profits. It is our joint responsibility to protect human values from deterioration, no matter, whether one is a technologist, an engineer, a teacher, a saint, a farmer and so on.

Most of us must be remembering the famous Hindi story entitled "*Haar ki Jeet*" wherein the saint Baba Bharti was deceived by a robber Khadga Singh by pretending to be a wounded person. Baba then requested the robber not to disclose this incident to anyone, or else the people would stop helping the needy ones, even if the case was very genuine. Baba Bharti of this story could probably be one of the examples of highest order having a deep concern for humanity, human values and the society as a whole.

Technological Progress and Unhealthy Practices

The world witnessed tremendous progress in almost all branches of science and technology; it may be the computer science and information technology, paint and plastic technology, biotechnology, environmental technology, energy, drugs and pharmaceuticals, aerospace engineering, agriculture, etc. It is good that most of these advancements are being done with almost a sole objective of welfare of the human beings, irrespective of a society/country, caste, colour, creed or religion. It is very satisfying that the scientists and technologists are toiling hard day and night to contribute something to the human welfare. In the field of medical sciences, commendable achievements have been claimed. But sometimes the output of their efforts is misused, and the boons turn into curses. Who will forget the boon of Einstein turned into a curse for Hiroshima..?

For the growth of business, all possible ways and means — wrong or right — are being practised today. Human welfare has been kept aside and has remained no more a point of discussion. Organisers of this seminar deserve a special thankfulness of the society for providing a platform for us to discuss such an important aspect of life. In the past, however, the considerations for honesty and human welfare used to enjoy a unique status and respect amongst all attributes of human life. A well-known saying "Salute the Rising Sun" is being badly misinterpreted today, as the definition of 'Sun' has been totally distorted from its original form.

To lead a luxurious life and the temptation for having physical things have become the dominant factors today in the society. As a result, all sorts of dirty games have crept into the technology-based business. We are not able to get fresh air to respirate and pure water to drink. Therefore, it has become essential now to analyse seriously our intentions behind the inventions, and to ascertain the right uses of the right technologies developed. Who doesn't know the good and bad points behind use of chemical fertilizers, drugs, allopathic medicines, etc.? Going back to the past, the practice of use of organic manure, naturopathy and yogabhyas seems to be one of the solutions. Let us thoroughly recapiturate our past, the old traditions and definitions, and assess now, as what are we heading to at present, and what are we going to be in the future. This could be understood only when we are able to understand explicitly the objective of our life.

The Objective of Human Life

No one can argue on the fact that every one must work hard sincerely for the welfare of one's family, state, country and the world as a whole. The children are taught today the ways and means by which they can earn money to fetch prosperity. They are educated in very clear terms as they should beat their rivals in any field, by hooks or by crooks. Studies on management also move around this. For material gains, they are hardly bothered as how much they have lost on human values, social values and, above all, the mental peace. They are forced to inculcate in their minds that life is only a competition, a war that you have to win somehow, and hence the people today have become extremely selfish and self-centred.

I want to pose two questions here before you to enable us understand the ultimate objective of our life:

Q.1.: What are we trying to achieve ultimately? To accumulate money and matter or to have a peace of mind?

Q.2.: At what cost, we are accumulating physical things? At the cost of our mental peace or at the cost of our commitment for our families and the society as a whole?

Based on the answers to these two fundamental questions, we can easily fix up our final goal of life. Someone may, however, misargue by saying, "I want to accumulate money for mental peace". As a matter of fact, the most funny confusion that we have in mind is that we are trying to get physical comforts and mental peace by sacrificing our physical comforts and mental peace of day and night. Friends, that is totally impossible, and hence we should pause and ponder to decide our right course of actions.

Factors Influencing Human Values

We, indeed, have advanced to a high level today technologically, but there is no doubt that the human values have been influenced significantly by our technological progress, westernisation of life style and the socio-economic and political conditions along with the government policies.

This is the age of computers and information technology. The computers have been established to be boon for our technological progress, as it has remarkably enhanced our knowledge of the latest range of products available in the market. This has resulted in us a strong temptation to bring home the latest things, causing serious dissatisfaction, and hence people do not hesitate to get them by wrong ways also.

For entertainment in the past, people used to assemble at one place, used to sing and dance together. In those days, they, however, didn't have effective means of exchanging information globally, and their general awareness and the rate of increase of knowledge was limited, but they were quite happy and mentally satisfied to lead peaceful living. Now, we have beautiful colour TV sets at our homes connected to a number of channels and the Internet connections, which have cut off the people from rest of the society, and hence the concern for mutual welfare is gradually weakened. There can be numerous such examples of our technological progress, which have attacked badly on human values.

In India, electronic media giving countless programmes, based on westernised culture, have made our children intolerant, violent, fashion-loving and highly ambitious. In the present time, you may find many highly ambitious persons saying "I will not be able to go to see my ailing mother admitted in ICU after her massive cardiac attack, as I have got an important business discussion". Yes, everybody can understand that this person is too much bothered for beating his professional rivals but doesn't bother at all about beating of his mother's heart. Friends, let us think and analyse whether this kind of thinking is right or wrong, and to what extent it is right in today's perspective.

Some of the government policies like reservation in India are not being properly implemented, and hence the needy talents are deprived of their due share in the society, causing in them an acute frustration. How can a frustrated talent with empty stomach think of human values or social values? We are, however, quite optimistic that the recently announced government recommendations for the teachers of degree-giving institutions (providing a sort of flexible structure for promotion of the teachers) will prove helpful in reducing the leg-pulling practices which are extremely detrimental for research and academics in the colleges and technological institutions, and ultimately retard the technological progress of the country.

Conclusion

It is necessary to emphasise that we must take specific lessons from our past and the experiences, improve upon, practise them at present, and strive hard for establishing the ideals of human values in all walks of life, including the technological progress. We should be bold enough in saying "no" to any or all such technologies, the progress of which is detrimental to humanity and human values.

To conclude, we can say that the litmus test as to what is to be developed technologically in India is contained in the Gandhiji's Talisman printed on NCERT books, which conveys the message that you should ensure, before developing any technology, that it must benefit the poorest person of the society you have ever met.

6

Integration of Human Values in Technological Progress

K.K. Ghosh

Scientific and technological progress is the blissful result of a thoughtful synthesis of technology transfer and the concept of TQM. While the technology transfer is essentially accomplished in three stages of invention, innovation and dissemination; the importance of TQM lies in articulating technology transfer practices in an eco-friendly manner. One important requirement of TQM would be amongst others, a balanced manpower development by acquisition of appropriate technical expertise and temper together with self and/or personality development.

Education in human values can, indeed, draw out the best in an individual to enable his personality to develop to perfection. This process of evolution of human excellence calls for excellence in each of five domains or aspects of human personality. These five domains, namely, physical, intellectual, emotional, physic and spiritual define the human system in-toto.

Five basic values, namely, truth, righteous conduct, peace, love and non-violence correspond to human personality and human values as mentioned in Fig. 6.1.

Since human beings everywhere in the world are alike, each can aspire to inculcate and internalize these values. These values are, thus, universal and transcend all distinctions of countries, religion, caste and creed.

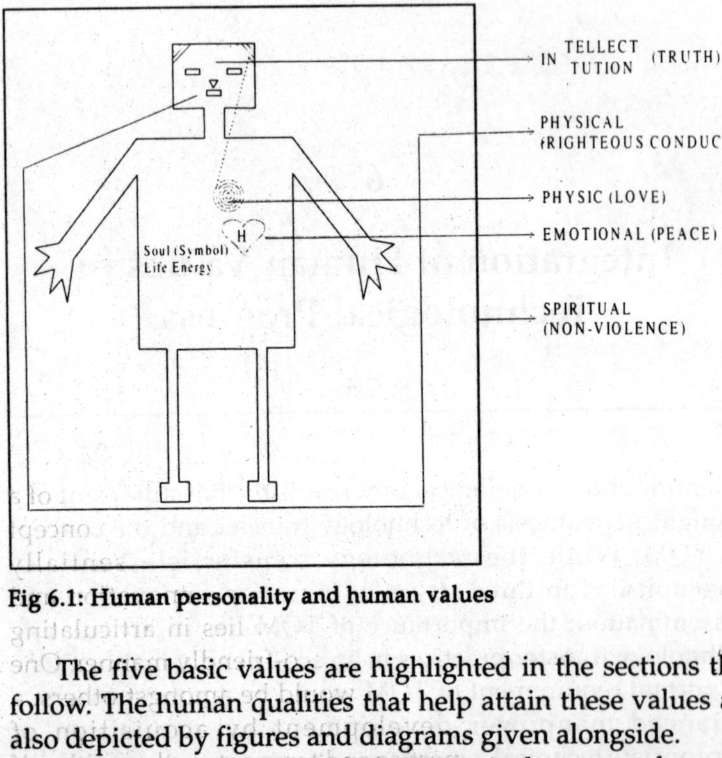

Fig 6.1: Human personality and human values

The five basic values are highlighted in the sections that follow. The human qualities that help attain these values are also depicted by figures and diagrams given alongside.

Finally, approaches to education in human values are highlighted.

Truth

The life principle within each of us is the truth. We would not be existent without it. This life principle is identified as the human soul which is in turn the resident divinity within each individual. It is this truth which is the basis of every other things and with the power of which the heart beats, the lungs breath and the system works. The role of human intellect is to find out the truth.

Interestingly, when one realises and experiences this truth, one sees that the same truth pervades every other person and object. And in essence we are all one.

Truth has different levels. There is the truth of sense perception, such as 'the fire burns'. One can ascertain this with one's senses. There is also the truth by inference, such as 'man is mortal'. We base this statement on the strength of our observation of those around us and extend it to arrive at a general conclusion, even though we may not have seen every human being born in this world dying. Apart from all these is the truth which is incapable of being destroyed or hurt. It persists and pervades the whole cosmos. The various truth levels are shown in Fig. 6.2.

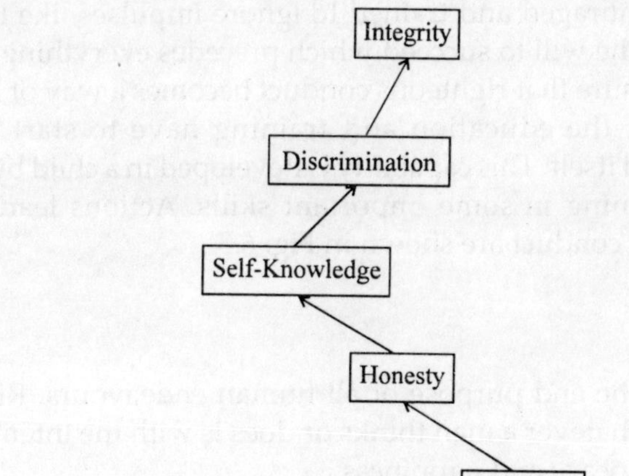

Fig. 6.2: Truth levels

Righteous Conduct

Truth in action is righteous conduct. The action takes place on the physical domain and behind each action there is thought. If this thought derives its sustenance from the human will, as opposed to human desire, the resultant action will be righteous.

What is of significance here is to understand the distinction between will and desire. 'Will' is the colourless component of human resolve which motivates and inspires him to act in accordance with the truth. Difference from this is the desire that prompts action. More often than not, this desire springs out from some myopic assumption or misbelief. The child has to be encouraged and trained to ignore impulses like this. In fact, it is the will to succeed which precedes everything else.

To ensure that righteous conduct becomes a way of life for a person, the education and training have to start in the childhood itself. This capability is developed in a child by some basic training in some important skills. Actions leading to righteous conduct are shown in Fig. 6.3.

Peace

Peace is the end purpose of all human endeavours. Right or wrong, whatever a man thinks or does is with the intention of attaining peace and happiness.

Peace would certainly become a far more attainable entity, if one were to know the domain of personality at which it is acquired.

It is only when there is an emotional equilibrium that one experiences peace. This equipoise is not inert or vegetative but a dynamic realisation that the emotional conflict and upsurge can never withstand the test of truth and righteousness. Peace is a state of 'power-packed stillness' and follows the awareness that the source of human fulfilment is within.

Often dubbed as a mirage, peace can be a reality for each of us if we have faith in our innate power to do good, to be good and see good.

What is equally important is to recognise that nothing in this universe is ever responsible for absence of peace within us. It is only when our internal emotional system is disturbed that

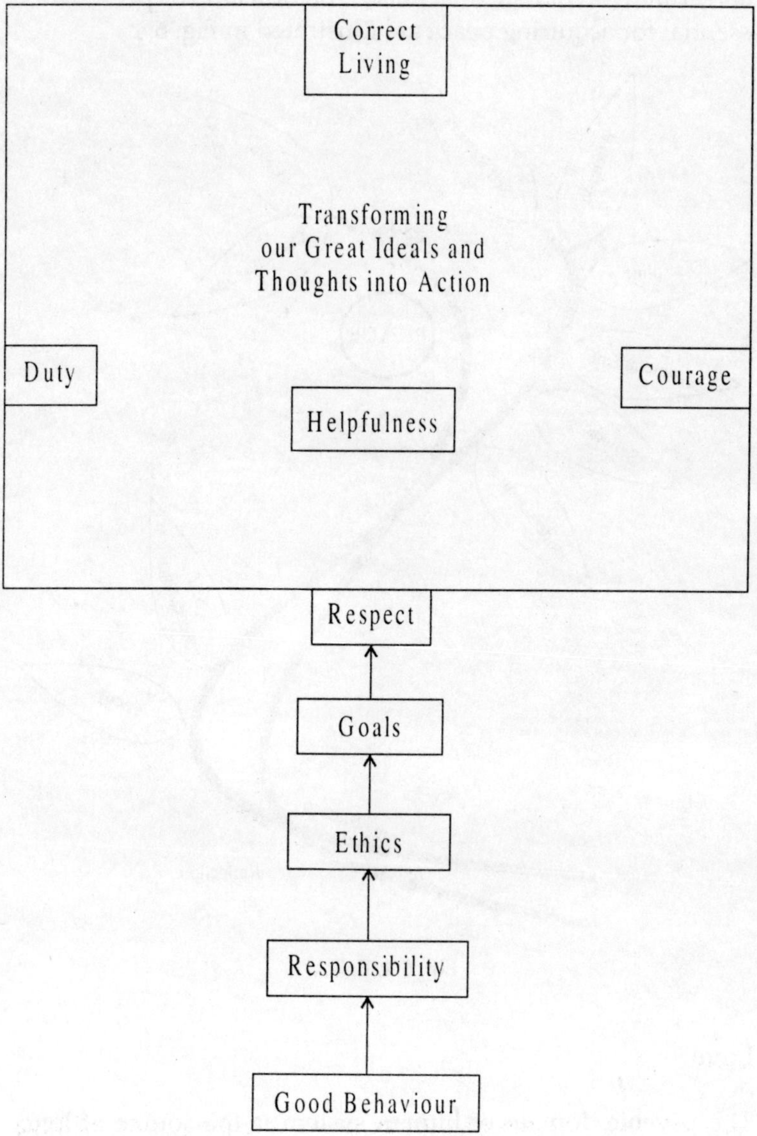

Fig. 6.3: Right Action

restlessness and confusion find a home. By conscious efforts we can certainly avoid such lacunae. The domains of personality essential for acquiring peace are illustrated in Fig. 6.4.

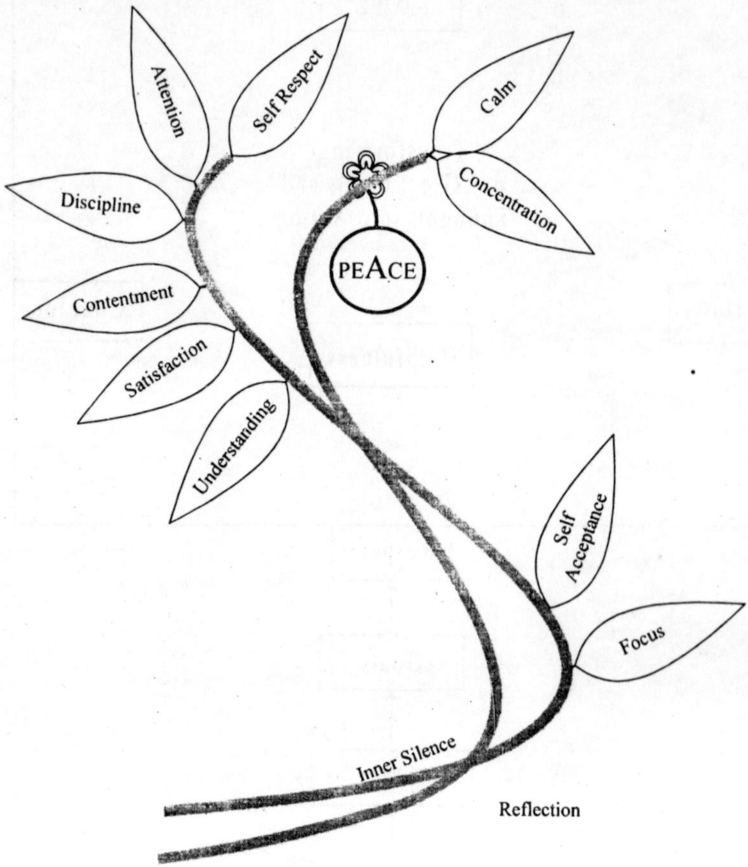

Fig. 6.4: Peace

Love

The psychic domain of human system is the source of love. Love is the expression of the individual divine within and is the power of soul. It is the mightiest of forces in the world and is truly representative of human nature.

Love is not an emotion. It is a form of energy which each individual transmits and receives every moment. It affects all forms of life. It is a peculiar possession which grows with sharing.

Love is the answer to the question; 'what in me loves — what in another person'. It is the reflection of the same truth that one loves. What to say of children, even animals and beasts respond to this power of love. Love helps us overcome the sense of fear by promoting better understanding and appreciation. Since love springs from the truth, it is in nature of righteous action and results in peace.

Love has to begin by manifesting itself towards parents and grow and graduate to include family, neighbourhood, country and most of all God. The journey to love can best be appreciated by the depiction in Fig. 6.5.

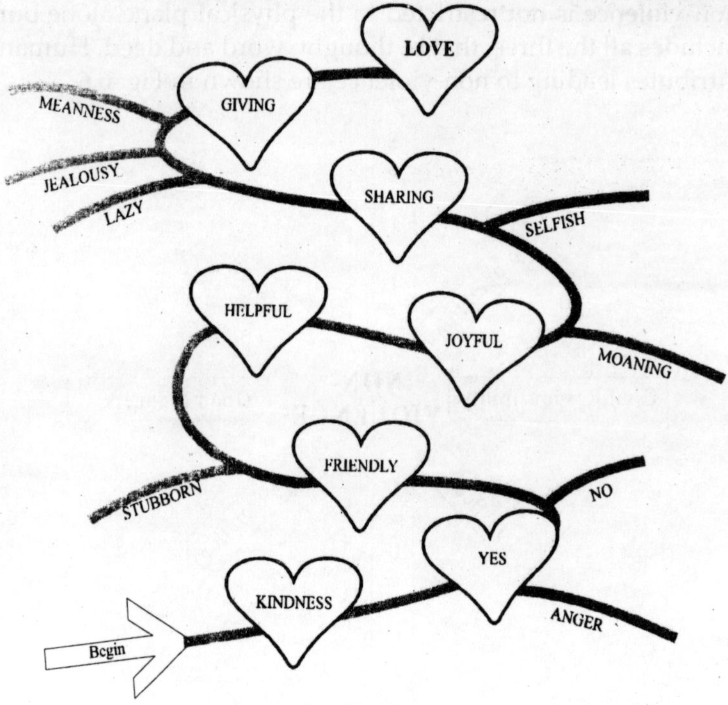

Fig. 6.5: Love

Non-violence

Non-violence is the zenith of human achievement and perfection. It is universal love that goes beyond our relation with our fellow beings and embraces all living and non-living things. It is the spiritual domain of existences. Here, one experiences the essential oneness and unity of all creation. It blossoms from the understanding that man has an obligation towards every object and component of this universe. And the least one can do is to try and extend one's sphere of love to all.

In the context of human being, non-violence means amity, harmony and the understanding; in the context of plants and animals it means non-injury, that is desisting from avoidable harm; and in the context of nature as such, it means non-violation of the law and balance of nature. Thus the practice of non-violence is not restricted to the physical plane alone but includes all the three, that is, thought, word and deed. Human attributes leading to non-violence are shown in Fig. 6.6.

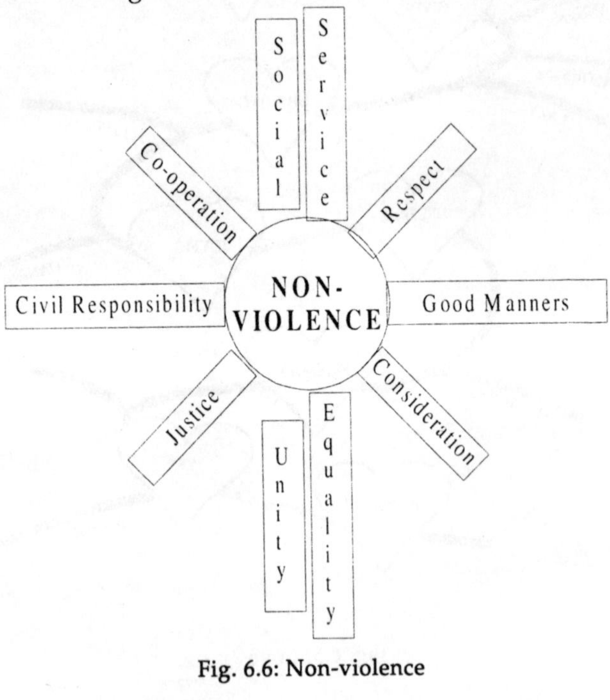

Fig. 6.6: Non-violence

Approaches to Education in Human Values

The five basic human values, as we have described above, are attainable through education. Approaches to education in human values are depicted in Fig. 6.7. Integration of human values in curricular and co-curricular works and also, in school subjects will be a viable step towards educating children in these lines. Besides, the knowledge of the above five human values can also be inducted to the minds of children through a direct way. This includes a posture of silent sitting, story telling, prayers, group singing and group activities. The knowledge of basic human values to children at school level may cause a reflective impact on their future life while they will be dealing with scientific and technological activities.

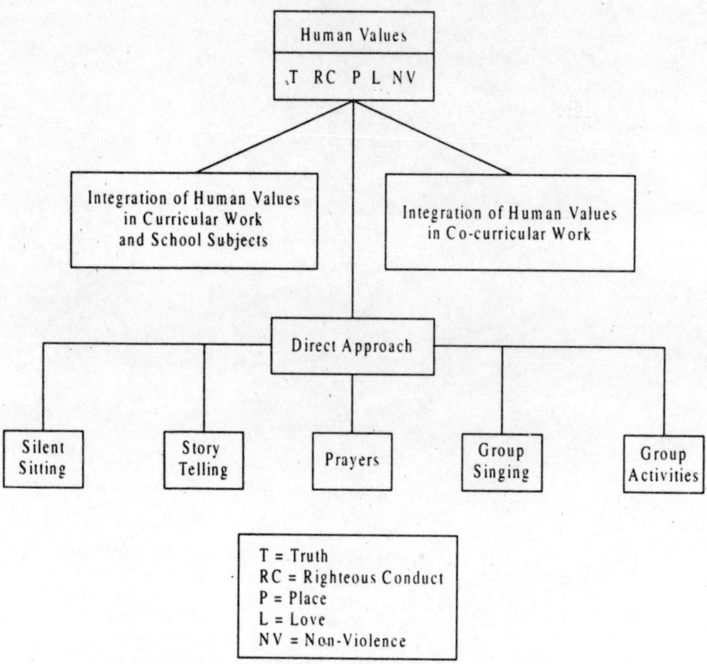

Fig. 6.7: Approaches to Education in Human Values

References

'The Beacon' published by World Council of Stir Satya Sai Organisation.
Howard Murphet, *SAI BABA: Invitation to Glory*, MacMillan India Ltd.
We Devotes.... Sri Satya Sai Books and Publication Trust.
Chinna Katha-I Sri Satya Sai Books and Publication Trust.
Dr. M.V.N. Murthy, *The Greatest Adventure*, Sri Satya Sai Books and Publication Trust.

SECTION II

A HARMONY BETWEEN 'MATERIALISM' AND 'SPIRITUALISM' THROUGH AN APPROPRIATE TECHNOLOGICAL REVOLUTION

7

Mind and Matter Conjuction in Maximization of Satisfaction

An Economic Analysis

K.M. Mohapatra and *V.K. Jain*

Introduction

In philosophical term, 'mind' is the seat of consciousness, thought and feeling. It is a non-physical part of a living being through which the 'soul' reveals itself and realises facts. 'Matter', on the other hand, is purely a physical part. When a living being clings to matters for enjoyment and pleasure, it applies its mind. Desires are reflected through mind. Pleasure from fulfilment of a desire depends upon how are the mind and the matter conjucted and what are their conditions at that movement. Satisfaction ('utility' in economics) to a person is the resultant of a simultaneous function of 'mind' and 'matter' or say, 'subject' and 'object'. Metaphysical relation is the base of utility analysis in economics.

For illustrating 'utility' principles, economists have assumed that the prospective consumer must be rational. He must have the mental state as to properly judge and compare utility levels obtained separately from different consumptions of goods available to him. Herein, 'mind' is implicitly presumed as distinct and independent of goods (matter). 'Utility' of a piece of goods to a consumer is determined jointly both by goods' quantity and quality and consumer's mental state. If the piece of goods is constant but the mental state of the consumer changes, the utility level tends to vary, or if the mental state of the consumer is fixed but the piece of goods changes, the 'utility' also varies. The function of 'mind' is important in determination of 'utility' of goods. The economists did not discuss much about this subject while they built utility models. The cardinalists (William Stanley Jevon, Leon Walras and Alfred Marshall, etc.) were of the view that 'utility' was measurable just as the weight of an object, and the quantity of an object determined 'utility'. On the other hand, the ordinalists (J.R. Hicks, P.A. Samuelson, E.E. Slutsky, H. Theil, etc.) vehemently objected the cardinal utility, and provided ordinal approach to utility analysis. According to them, 'utility' was not measurable in absolute term, but a rational consumer could compare and rank utility that he obtained from consumption of various bundles of goods. A consumer could reveal his preference for a bundle of goods on the basis of its utility to him. The ordinal approach to utility was considered to be more logical and scientific than the cardinal approach. However, both approaches had certain common implications. 'Mind', 'utility' and 'goods', being three separate entities, were common to both. Whether 'utility' was cardinal or ordinal, as implied, it was mainly the function of physical quantity of goods. The role of 'mind' in determination of 'utility' was neglected by the economists. Truly, 'utility' of a thing is not at all independent of 'mind'. The state of 'mind' of a consumer cannot be assumed to be unchanged. If the mental state of a consumer differs, the same bundle of goods may give him different levels of utility. Under this situation, the assumptions of consumer consistency and transitivity are to be violated. The efficacy of ordinal utility laws will be nowhere.

The welfare economic models based on utility principles would also be put to the same objections from metaphysical angles. For maximization of social welfare, the cardinalists considered equal distribution of income among all individuals in a society as an important criterion whereas the ordinalists emphasised both the equal distribution of income as well as the efficient allocation of resources. In ordinal approaches (Kaldor: 1939, Hicks: 1939, Bergson: 1938, Lipsey and Lancaster: 1957, Samuelson: 1966, Winch: 1971, Sen: 1973, etc.), the value judgement of alternative sets of economic arrangements for social welfare was implicit in some cases and explicit in others. Many admitted that in a society, if a set of economic policy arrangements made some people better-off and some others worse-off, and thereafter, there was net betterment to the society, that would indicate an increase of social welfare. For judging between 'better-off' and 'worse-off' of various groups of people in a society, the economists would adopt the 'utility norms'. By and large, in welfare economic studies, value judgement (or utility judgement) was the main exercise. The mental state of all members of the society, along with their physical possessions, would determine the social welfare, which was rarely considered. In economic models, the discussion of non-physical part (mental state), which is now very crucial, is not generally covered perhaps due to its non-quantifiability. Only increasing or rearranging of physical entities would not be sufficient condition for maximization of social welfare. The mental condition of a society's members plays vital role in social utility determination. The non-physical factors such as freedom, security, peace, environment, etc. significantly contribute to social welfare. Because these factors influence the state of mind of the people.

Our present model exhibits a trial of linking physical to non-physical factors for utility analysis and describing social welfare as well. This is an attempt to redress the models of utility and social welfare in terms of a metaphysical perception: mind and matter conjuction. This paper consists of five sections.

SECTION I: MIND AND MATTER CONJUCTION

As we have said earlier, the 'utility' of an object (matter) to an individual depends upon its interaction with individual's subject (mind). So that we write as follows:

$$U_{x_1c_1} = f(o_{x_1} \leftarrow m_{c_1})$$

$U_{x_1c_1}$ = total utility of x_1 object to c_1 consumer

o_{x_1} = quantity and quality of object x_1 available to c_1 consumer

m_{c_1} = state of mind of c_1 consumer

$(o_{x_1} \leftarrow m_{c_1})$ = conjuction of mind of c_1 consumer with x_1 object

Let in a society there is *n* number of objects, *i.e.* x_1, x_2, ... x_n and *k* number of persons, *i.e.* c_1, c_2, ... c_k. Then, the social utility can be expressed as follows:

Total utility of c_1 person for *n* number of objects is:

$$\sum_{i=1}^{n} U_{x_1c_1} = f(o_{x_1} \leftarrow m_{c_1}) + f(o_{x_2} \leftarrow m_{c_1}) + ... + f(o_{x_n} \leftarrow m_{c_1})$$

Total utility of *k* number of persons for *n* number of objects is:

$$\begin{bmatrix}\text{Total}\\ \text{social}\\ \text{utility}\end{bmatrix} = U_s = \sum_{\substack{i=1\\ j=1}}^{nk} U_{x_ic_j} = \sum_{j=1}^{k} f(o^*_{x_1} \leftarrow m_{c_1}) + \sum_{j=1}^{k} f(o^*_{x_2} \leftarrow m_{cj})$$

$$+ .... + \sum_{j=1}^{k} f(o^*_{x_n} \leftarrow m_{c_j})$$

[$o^*_{x_i}$ = sum of o_{x_i} objects available to *k* individuals]

$\sum_{j=1}^{n} f(o^*_{x_1} \leftarrow m_{c_j})$ = total satisfaction of the society from object x_1.

$\sum_{j=1}^{k} f(o^*_{x_2} \leftarrow m_{c_j})$ = total satisfaction of the society from object x_2 and so on.

This can be reduced to:

$$\begin{bmatrix}\text{Total}\\ \text{social}\\ \text{utility}\end{bmatrix} = U_s = \sum_{i=1}^{n}\sum_{j=1}^{k} f(o^*_{x_{ij}} \leftarrow m_{c_{ij}})$$

$$= \sum_{i=1}^{n}\left[\sum_{j=1}^{k} f(o^*_{x_j}) \leftarrow \sum_{j=1}^{k} f(m_{c_s})\right]$$

$$= \underbrace{\sum_{i=1}^{n}\sum_{j=1}^{k} f(o^*_{x_{ij}})}_{\text{Total Object Function}} \leftarrow \underbrace{\sum_{i=1}^{n}\sum_{j=1}^{k} f\left(m_{c_{ij}}\right)}_{\text{Total mental Function}}$$

Since 'object' and 'mind' are independent to each other, an segregation of 'object' and mental state of all individuals in a society is possible.

Total social satisfaction (U_s) will be conjuction of total mental function of the society with its total object function. For simplicity, we call 'total mental function' as Society Mental Force (SMF) and, 'total object function' (total of want satisfying capacity of objects) as Society Object Force (SOF). For maximization of total social satisfaction (social welfare), a well conjuction between SMF and SOF is necessary. This is explained with the help of Fig. 7.1

Starting with point e_1 on *OA* (SOF and SMF equalizing line), we observe that SOF is equal to SMF. We call this as conjuction of SMF and SOF. This conjuction is natural because it is achieved through the process of natural growth of the society. We call it as *natural conjuction point*. Corresponding to this conjuction point, Society Total Satisfaction (STS) is maximum at point 'm_1' on STS_1 (Society Total Satisfaction curve). STS curve is concave to X-axis due to the law of diminishing marginal utility. This is natural maximization of society's satisfaction.

Below or above OO_1 level of SOF, a conjuction between SMF and SOF is possible but through the process of changing the SMF. For example, at OO_3 level of SOF, the SMF is greater than the SOF by I_3e_3 magnitude. This means that actual amount of physical things being available to individuals is not adequate to meet their minimum desires as per their mental levels. So that they feel scarcity of objects, and the scarcity creates tension

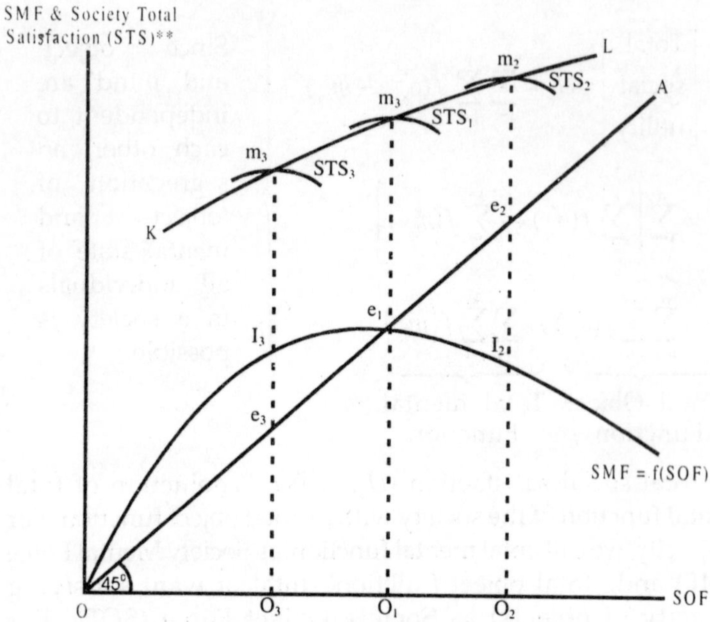

Fig. 7.1: Determinants of SMF and Society Total Satisfaction.

Note: If SMF = f(SOF) and socio-cultural and ethical values are unchanged, then.

$$\text{SMF}^* = \begin{bmatrix} \text{Increasing function of (SOF)} & \text{limited to } O_1 \text{ level of SOF} \\ \text{Decreasing function of (SOF)} & \text{beyond } O_1 \text{ level of SOF} \end{bmatrix}$$

* At the lower level of SOF, SMF is lower because lower quantum of physical things in proportion to desires of individuals creates scarcity, and scarcity and deprivation lower down mental state of the individuals. SMF increases along with an increase in SOF. This is so because as SOF increases due to economic development (growth of physical entities), SMF starts to increase due to fulfillment of individuals minimum desires. After certain level of SOF, say, beyond 'O_1' in the diagram, SMF decreases corresponding to each increase in SOF. This is due to the fact that when the total force of physical entities exceeds the force of individuals' desires (as per social norms), SOF will cause adverse impact on the mental state of individuals (discussed later) which will lower down SMF. Therefore, SMF curve is concave to the X-axis.

** STS curve is concave to X-axis due to law of diminishing marginal utility. It shifts upward as social mental force (SMF) improves with an increase of social object force (SOF).

in the state of minds of the individuals. Under the condition of SMF-SOF disequilibrium, the Society Total Satisfaction (STS) could not be maximized. In order to maximize STS, there are two alternative options: (i) pull down the SMF curve to the point e_3 where there will be conjuction between SOF and SMF or (ii) expand the SOF (physical entities) to the level O_1 where the society will have natural conjuction between SOF and SMF. For the first option, socio-cultural and ethical revolution is required which could create a condition for the individuals for self-containment of minds under which their desires are to be reduced to the availability of physical things. This action would bring about a shift in SMF curve, which would pass through point e_3. Corresponding to the point of conjuction e_3, the society would maximize satisfaction at point m_3, i.e. the maximum point on STS_3 curve. But the maximum of STS with OO_3 of SOF is relatively lower than the maximum of STS with OO_1 of SOF. The conjuction could not be a permanent one. Because, at this point of conjuction, the human desires are suppressed through self-containment of their minds, which is not natural of all ordinary human beings. This suppression of desires is temporary in a dynamic society. Thus, we call 'e_3' as instable conjuctive point.

Let SOF be expanded to OO_2 level through technological break-through in the fields of production and investment (in physical entities) and kept socio-cultural and ethical (non-physical) conditions of the society unchanged. At this level, the SMF is lower than the SOF by the magnitude of e_2I_2. This means that availability of physical things in the society is much greater than the society's minimum desires as per social norms. This condition will cause to an emergence of evil desires (discussed later) in human minds. An excess of physical resources in proportion to a human's mental level often induce him to misuse (or overuse) resources as his passions and ego (all sort of vices) start to develop under this condition. Consequently, this trend in human leads him towards moral and social degradations which adversely affect the human mental stage. At OO_2 level of SOF, the society may not maximum STS under the stationary condition of socio-cultural and ethical values. In order to maximize STS, there are again two alternative options: (i) cut down SOF to point O_1 level for maximum social satisfaction at point, m_1, or (ii) if the development of SOF is to be sustained at point O_2, then SMF curve is to be pushed up to point e_2, where SOF will have well conjuction with SMF. For this, SMF curve will be shifted upward. This action of pushing of SMF upward is feasible through the process of socio-cultural and ethical revolution under which influence the noble desires in human will be highly active and evil desires in him will be eliminated. The society would avail maximum satisfaction at point m_2. The society's maximum satisfaction at point m_2 will be much higher than that at point m_1. The conjuction between SMF and SOF at point e_2 is supernatural because in ordinary society this conjuction is less possible. We call this point e_2 as supernatural conjuctive point.

If the points of social satisfaction maxima are connected across various STS curves, we shall get an expansion path for a society for welfare maximization through the process of well conjucting between SMF and SOF at different stages of development. KL curve is the expansion path for maximization of social welfare.

SECTION II: DETERMINANTS OF SOCIETY MENTAL FORCE

Society mental force (SMF) means mental state of its all individual members. The mental state of an individual depends on many factors. As told earlier, 'soul' of an individual reveals its desires and realises satisfaction through its mind (a non-physical part). A mind acts with the help of its brain (a physical part in human). An important factor which influences the state of mind of an individual is the nature of relation between his 'subject' and 'object' or say his 'desires' and 'means'. If a human's 'means' is adequate to meet his 'desires' in a time, his mental state remains undisturbed. If there is clash between 'desires' and 'means', his mental state is disturbed and weakened. In this sense, the physical things (objects) influence the mental condition of the human being. Besides this, there are many other factors (see Fig. 7.2) which may influence the mental state of a human. Some of them are explained below:

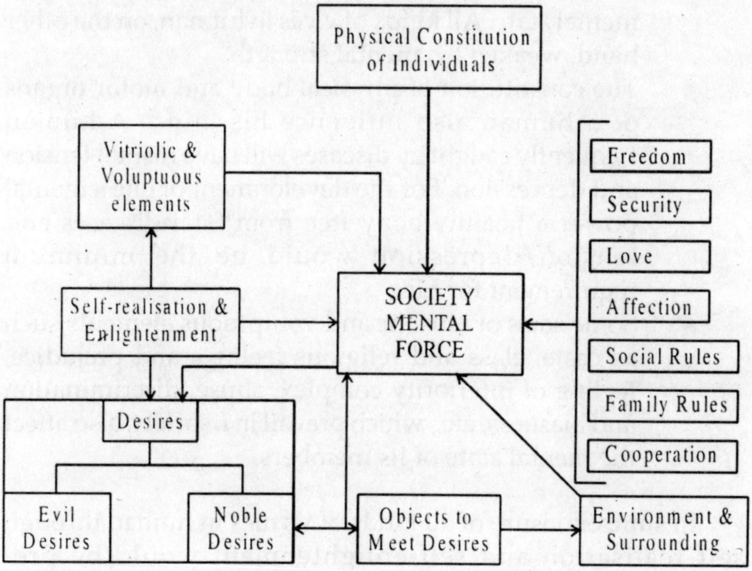

Fig. 7.2: Determinants of Society Mental Force (SMF)

- The nature of desires originating from one's mind indirectly influences his mental state. A person's evil desires and actions often put him in physical and mental troubles whereas his noble desires and actions provide him with mental satisfaction and peace.
- The social and family rigid rules often affect the state of mind of an individual.
- Self-enlightenment through education and intuition causes modification and refinement in the state of one's mind. Self-enlightenment and self-realisation in human raise the level of his consciousness.
- The surroundings and environment of a human being are important factors which greatly influence his mental state.
- The freedom and security to a human life are

considered to be necessary conditions for the development of his mental state.

- Love, affection, kindness, forgiveness, etc. are all sorts of virtues in human, which largely contribute to his mental state. All kinds of vices in human, on the other hand, weaken his mental strength.
- The constitution of physical body and motor organs of a human also influence his mind. A human frequently caught by diseases will have mental tension and depression. For the development of one's mental power a healthy body free from fatal diseases and tension/depression would be the minimum requirement for him.
- Some sorts of vitriolic and voluptuous elements such as caste, class and religious feelings and prejudice, feeling of inferiority complex, abuse, discrimination and biasness, etc., which prevail in a society, also affect the mental state of its members.

In sum, exposure of all kinds of virtues in human through self-realisation and self-enlightenment would be pre-requirements for the development of a society's mental force.

SECTION III: DETERMINENTS OF SOCIETY OBJECT FORCE

A society's object force depends upon the availability of goods and services in a time. Human desires initially determine what to be produced and at what quantity. Later on, his some desires get induced due to a change in his living style. For production in order to match with human desires, a producer adopts typical technology depending on resource availability and scientific knowledge. Entrepreneurship in the field of production is one of the important parameters of physical development of the society. More investment in production generates more employment (within a given technological setup). More employment provides more purchasing power to individuals, which meet their desires. Since human desires are unlimited and there is also no limit to producer's expectations for profits, an unabated increase in consumption-produciton process may lead to mass production and mass exploitation of natural resources. So that the society object force expands. A growth process can be led by two circular ways: (i) human desires → invention of technology → production → employment-income → human desires, and (ii) invention of technology → production → employment-income → human desires → invention of technology (see Fig. 7.3). In the first process, human desires take active part whereas technology takes passive role. In the second process, technology plays key role and human desires play passive role. In the second process, desires are inducted in human by the producers through advertisement and demonstrations.

A social change causes changes in human desires. A social change takes place due to three reasons: as exclusively endogenous change, particularly a change in thoughts of human through self-enlightenment, without coming into the influence of outside socio-culture, gives birth to a social revolution; (ii) an exclusively exogenous change pervading to a society causes its socio-cultural change; and (iii) a partly endogenous and partly exogenous change may bring about a mixing change in a society. If a social change originates exclusively from endogenous factors, then the human desires in the society take active role in the developmental process. In this case, the development of science and technology becomes derivative of people's desires. What people desire, science and technology is mooted accordingly. Mostly, the developmental process in European and American societies was the example of this kind. On the other hand, if a change in a society is due to, partly or wholly, the influence of exogenous change, then the science and technology take active role and the human desires take passive role in the development. Outward invention of technology pervades to a society where it was non-existent and creates desires in its inhabitants. In that sense, human desires are induced or motivated. In many instances, the development process in India is a typical example of this kind.

In sum, society object force is mainly determined by human desires, level of natural resources, science and technology, entrepreneurship and the process of development.

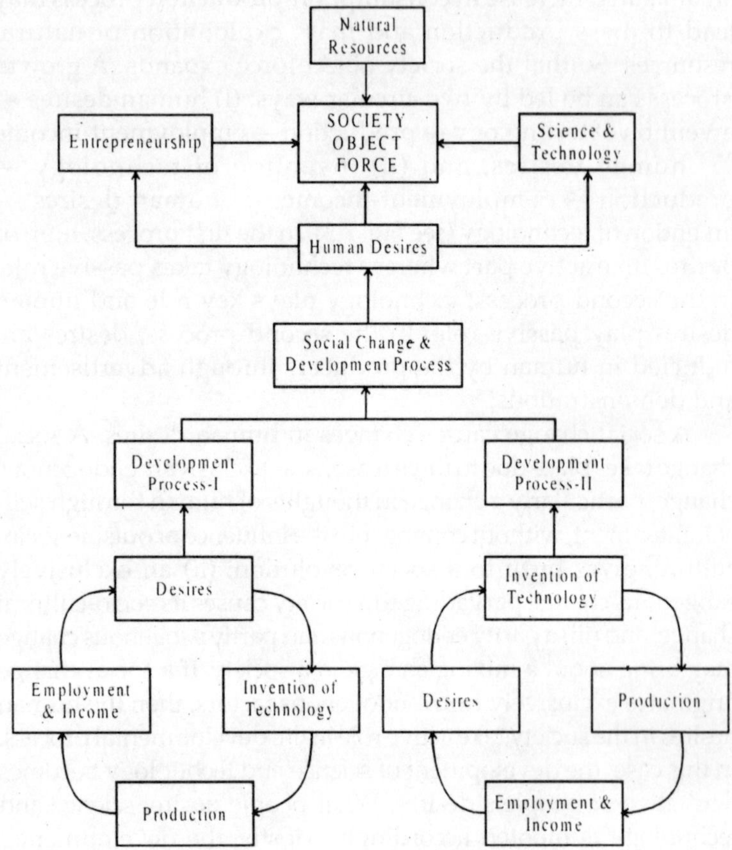

Fig. 7.3: Determinants of Society Object Force (SOF)

SECTION IV: ROLE OF SCIENCE & TECHNOLOGY IN CONJUCTION BETWEEN SMR & SOF

'Necessity is the mother of invention'. Human necessity and desires insist him to invent a mechanical process or a technique for production of desired objects. As we have said in previous section, wherever human desire has been the cause of a technological invention, the former takes active role and the latter is passive to play in the developmental process. This happens in a society where changes originate from endogenous source, not from the influence of outer systems. If an invention of technology is viewed for noble desires in human, that technology will have less adverse impacts on him as well as on his environment. By noble desires of human, we mean such wants of human which could be fulfilled without any indication of its adversity on him and on others, rather, the fulfilment of such desires can benefit others. In other words, these desires do not create any hazard to human morality nor to society. Such desires could indirectly be helpful in development of mental state of human. Any technological break-through meant for noble desires of human can bring about a well conjuction between 'mind' and 'matter'.

On the other hand, the evil desires in a human insist him to misuse an invention. By evil desires, we mean such wants of a human whose fulfilment may harm him or/and others' interests. For example, a nuclear technology, whenever it is used by the human for noble purpose, say, for energy generation, it may not have any apparent adverse impact on the mankind. But, whenever it is used by him as a weapon in a war, it will have adverse impact on the mankind as well as on its environment. Under this circumstance, it creates human and social hazards and the state of mind of the human is tensified. Similarly, a technology of computer virus is desired by a group of persons to damage the interest of some other groups of computer users. Such technological actions are due to evil desires in them. It creates worry in human mind. A number of similar examples can be cited in which a technological development is misused owing to evil desires of human. Under such situation, a technology could not maintain balance between human desires and its state of mind. The social welfare deteriorates due to a decrease in total human satisfaction.

Since invention of technology is linked to both noble desires as well as evil desires in human and, again, it is responsible for interlinking human desires to his mental conditions, it could be feasible on the part of scientists to cause favourable situation in the society through an appropriate technological revolution under which the evil desires in human would be suppressed and noble desires in him would develop. This situation will be favourable for the society for maximization of its welfare, hence it can bring about a well conjuction between noble desires and mental state of human at different stages of technological and scientific development.

SECTION V: CONCLUSION

By the large, for a sustainable development of a society in all directions, a well conjuction between 'mind' and 'matter' (between 'subject' and 'object') is logically justifiable. In economic study, for the objective of social welfare maximization, the issues relating to non-physical aspects should be equally stressed as is being done in physical aspects of development. For a balanced and sustainable development of the society, every increase in physical aspect should be conjucted with a corresponding increase in mental condition. We believe that a well conjuction between 'mind' and 'matter' can be established at every stage of development through an appropriate technological revolution along with socio-cultural and ethical changes which would suppress evil desires and cause noble desires to spring up in human.

In order to lead a human society towards the condition of maximum welfare, human value ought to be attached to economic criteria. An approach to equal distribution of income and efficient allocation of resources should be supplemented with the conditions of equality in non-physical things such as security, freedom, love, affection, emotion, tolerance, power, self-realisation, enlightenment, etc.

References

Bergson, A. (1938), "A Reformulation of Certain Aspects of Welfare Economics", *Quarterly Journal of Economics*, Vol. 52, January.

Hicks, J.R. (1939), "The Foundations of Welfare Economics", *Economic Journal*, pp. 696-712.

Hicks, J.R. (1946), "*Value and Capital*", 2nd ed., Clarendon Press, Oxford.

Kaldor, Nicholas (1939), "Welfare Propositions in Economics and

Interpersonal Comparisons of Utility", *Economic Journal*, Vol. XLIX.

Lipsey, R.G. and Kelvin Lancaster (1956-57), "The General Theory of Second Best", *Review of Economic Studies*, Vol. 24.

Marshall, Alfred (1920), *Principles of Economics*, 8th ed., Macmillan, London.

Samuelson, P.A. (1948), *Foundations of Economic Analysis*, Harvard University Press, Cambridge.

Samuelson, P.A. (1966), *Collected Scientific Papers*, Ed. by J.E. Stiglitz, Cambridge, Mass: M.I.T., 2 Vols.

Sen, Amartya (1973), *On Economic Inequality*, Clarendon Press, Oxford.

Slutsky, E.E. (1915), On the Theory of Budget of the Consumer, *Giornale Degil Economisti*, Vol. 51, July pp. 1-26, reprinted in American Association, Reading in Price Theory, Homewood - III Irwin, 1952.

Theil, H. (1975), *Theory and Measurement of Consumer Demand*, Amsterdam, North Holland.

Walras, Leon (1954), *Elements of Pure Economics*, Trans. Jaffe, Allen and Unwin.

Winch, D.M. (1971), *Analytical Welfare Economics*, Penguin.

8

Technological Progress
At What Cost?

G. Vidyanath and *I. Ramachandra Reddy*

One of the main indicators and means of economic growth in a developing economy like India is technological progress. According to dictionary, technological progress refers to a continuous growth or an advancement towards a goal or the developmental activity in science and technology, especially with reference to the commercial opportunities created thereby or to the promotion of the material well being of the public through the goods, techniques, facilities created or provided, etc. The above meaning indicates that there is a real technological progress only when it results in the welfare of the people through improvement of existing technology or techniques or facilities provided for living. Therefore, it is viewed as a right indicator of development of an economy, as it should contribute to the welfare of humanity at large and improves the quality of their living. Hence, the real technological progress should go hand-in-hand with the improvement of the quality of living in the same direction at the same pace.

Matter can neither be created nor be destroyed. With the help of technology, we can only change the already existing matter to create place utility, form utility and price utility. If the man is part of the nature, the man-made/man-discovered technology should also be part of the nature. Along with the creation of man, the technology to make his living possible must have also been created. The man, with the gifted intelligence, is only discovering and improving the already existing technology from time-to-time, as need arises, in order to improve the quality of living or the society. Therefore, any technological progress will be within the limits of the nature and it is only research and development of the nature by the man for improving the quality of his life. However, there is a standard equation of the nature for a given quality of our living with a little flexibility, *i.e.*, anything in excess in one place may lead to nearly proportionate shortage of something else in another place or too much of development in one area might have caused nearly proportionate underdevelopment in another area or behind every construction of something there is nearly proportionate destruction of something else. Therefore, any technological progress within that equation will improve the quality of our living. But when an imbalance in this equation is caused, the cost of the technological progress will be very high in terms of the quality of our life.

Therefore, today there is a need to ponder over the questions, such as:

(1) whether the technological progress today has improved the quality of our living? and
(2) what is the cost of technological progress in terms of the quality of life?

In this paper an humble attempt is made to assess the extent to which technological progress has hampered the improvement of the quality of our life by highlighting some of the areas, where its cost is higher than its contributions to the improvement of the quality of our living.

In history, we find that anything invented would be the part of history for some years, during which the man will search for its capacity to satisfy the human wants, then he will put it to the commercial use by giving it a value in terms of utility. This, in turn, should improve the quality of our living to some extent. Every product has a life cycle of four stages. In its first two stages, *i.e.*, introduction and growth, any improvement in it will improve the quality of life of the users while in its third stage, the saturation, we find that any further improvements made or facilities provided in it would not contribute anything positively to the quality of our living.

In other words, any instrument or a machine, or a home appliance, or a vehicle would perform well with a limited number of functions and if the number of functions or facilities were increased, the number of troubles would also increase proportionately or at a greater proportion. Today, our lives are no exception to this. The rapid technological progress around us has certainly improved the quality of our living to some extent, but beyond certain stage, it is felt that the quality of our life has suffered in many aspects of the life. Some of the important ones are:

(a) Technological Progress at the Cost of National Security

The technological progress should not be at the cost of the national security. The technological progress on defence front in one country should not provoke its neighbouring rival countries to counter it. The nuclear bomb is one of the milestones in the defence technological progress of our country. Besides, exhibiting our strength to withstand any kinds of attacks on us from enemies, the invention and testing of nuclear weapons will also be provoking our enemies to make a similar one or a more dangerous weapon. This in turn increases the threat to the human life, as our rival countries can also make and use same kind of bomb on us at anytime. For example, India and Pakistan have tested the nuclear bombs and now they are not able to get into an agreement on ethical grounds regarding the usage of the weapon.

(b) Technological Progress Leading to Rise in the Prices

Technological progress enables to discover new products to make our lives more comfortable. This will also increase the uses for which a basic raw material can be put to, thereby increasing the demand for it and making it all the more scarce commodity, which will in turn rise its price. Therefore, today, the common man is deprived of some of the essential goods, such as kerosene, cooking gas, diesel, petrol, etc., whose alternative uses have been multiplied with the technological progress. For example, today, usage of cooking gas for running a vehicle will rise its utility and makes it all the more scarce commodity and increases its price.

(c) Technological Progress at the Cost of Environment

The technological progress attained so far has increased speed of production in many sectors of our economy. As a result, we are able to get two or three crops in a year with the use of artificial fertilizers rather than using the natural manure. All of us, consuming such grains are only consuming more chemicals. Such food, instead of or besides providing energies, leads to some complications in the human constitution leading to chronic health problems. Another case of technological progress is the industrial development, which in many towns is leading to noise, air and ground water pollution, causing many chronic diseases to the people living in the surrounding areas. To use the improved technology, we need a lot of infrastructure, which will cost us too much in terms of environment, *i.e.*, deforestation on one hand and additional tax burden on the public on the other. With the help of technological progress today, we are able to pump out water, gas, crude oil, etc. from the earth at a very high speed. This is causing ecological imbalance and leading to natural calamities.

(d) Technological Progress Making the People Lethargic

Today, as the result of the technological progress, we feel that we can perform more than one function at a time and perform a function with a greater speed with the help of some devices, forgetting that many a products are designed by capitalizing our laziness. Because of usage of these products, the people are avoiding the basic movement of the human body leading to some health problems. For example, using products like washing machines, vacuum cleaners, mixers or grinders, etc., we are avoiding bending, grinding, swinging, etc. movements of our body. Because of lack of basic exercises, we are exposed to some chronic health problems, such as joint pains, blood pressure, etc.

(e) Technological Progress Increasing the Risk to the Life

In order to reduce the cost of production with the help of value analysis or value engineering, the manufacturers use lighter materials in manufacturing vehicles besides increasing their speed. As more power is packed in the lighter vehicles, the travelling become more risky and fatal. In most of the cases of accidents, heavy damage is caused to the vehicle and danger to the life of the rider.

(f) Technological Progress at the Cost of Affections

Another important landmark of the technological progress is the development of various means of communication. This made people to turn more artificially affectionate than naturally affectionate. Today, the world has become smaller and the people wish to reach each other through telephone or internet instead of visiting personally. Gradually, the affections will reduce and the people will be drawn apart. Visiting people once will increase the affections than just calling them.

(g) Technological Progress Leading to Under Utilisation of Man's Capacity

The power of the human brain is such that it gets sharpened only when it is used more and more. The students today are under utilising their mental capacities by depending more on the external mechanical/electronic devices. They are admiring at the capacity of a computer and forgetting the strength of human brain behind it. In other words, they are gaining computer confidence and loosing self-confidence. The technological progress has led the young people to use calculators for making simple calculations, increasing their dependence on these devises, and are getting addicted to these instruments; as a result, their mental abilities are getting rusted. They believe a machine but not themselves.

Due to technological development, today we are able to get many a television channels. Constantly watching of television, we are wasting a lot of time and becoming blind and lazy. In some cases of industries/organisations, many man-hours are also lost.

(h) Technological Progress at the Cost of Employment Opportunities

Our country is already facing the problem of unemployment. Adding to this, in most of the industries, replacing the human beings with computer-aided manufacturing machines increases the unemployment problem.

Another way of disemploying people is to force them to close whatever a small business they have. The developed technology is so costly and available only to big firms. As the small business firms cannot afford it they are forced to close their shops and perishing slowly.

Another way of technological progress affecting the quality of public life can be witnessed in public service department. Today, many of these departments are computerised. The people working in these departments are reluctant to work manually when the computers breake-down.

When the machines are working automatically, the people at the machines are idle mentally. In some of the industrial organizations, these idle minds are becoming the devil's workshops, by increasing the number of informal organisations, which in turn entertain the ideas of fighting for more pay, perks, privileges, besides the discussions on political and social scenario, etc., than working for more productivity and prosperity. This may lead to strikes, lockouts, closures of industrial organisations, etc.

(i) Technological Progress Changing the Direction of Human Life

The development of science will lead to the development of

technology. The science too has some boundaries, only within which the technology progresses. Today, the technological progress achieved seeds to have deviated the man from the purpose/goal of his life. With the help of scientific knowledge, we are learning a lot about the things which are already existing, the reasons for many diseases and even for the death, but failing to know about the creator and the purpose of life. Science can only provide medicines to relieve us from some worries temporarily but with some side effects. Science can make a person live for longer without much 'life' or 'the self' in living. Science is below the senses of organ or '*Indriyas*' and entertains them by providing the bodily happiness, but not happiness to the heart or 'the bliss' today. Because of scientific and technological progress, we are becoming more materialistic and immersed in temporary pleasures, and finally, forgetting the goal of life. The materialistic pleasures will also make us forget our rich Indian culture. These materialistic pleasures will provoke the people to play politics, by bringing down the human and ethical values. Finally, our lives are becoming so mechanical that we all are becoming vehicles without 'self start' and requiring a push every time we need to move. This is where the spirituality comes into picture. Spirituality starts where the science ends. Spiritual knowledge will enlightens anybody by explaining about the creator and the created. With the help of some spiritual exercises we can live longer and our life will be purposeful by making us realised and improved the 'self'. They can also relieve us from worries permanently and they also provide more resistance power. The happiness derived from the spiritual exercises will be permanent on the bliss. The development of spirituality will improve the human and ethical values in the society.

However, the technological progress is a must for the developing economy like ours, but it should contribute positively to the growth and development of ecological equation of the environment, the human, ethical and cultural values in the society, the intellectual ability, besides material welfare to the humanity at large. Scientific knowledge is must for our children, but it should develop their intellectual ability but not memory power. Scientific knowledge should give us the material benefits but it should not make us to forget the 'spirit' behind/beyond it.

Conclusion

In conclusion, any chronic disease can be diagnosed only in its third stage of growth, at which the chances of its cure are very remote, and thus we should continue to live in the same condition. If at all there are cases of coming back to life, they must be miracles of the divinity. Similarly, our dependence on mechanical/electronic devises has already reached its third stage, or probably in the beginning of the final stage. Therefore, we should try to control and counter it with the development of spirituality by tapping and strengthening our inner 'self' to improve the quality of our living.

9

Science, Spiritualism and Quality of Life

Geetanjali S. Patil

Science and Technology have always tried for the betterment of human being. Scientific and technological developments in the areas of food, clothing, housing, electricity, magnetism, communication, etc. have made possible for decreasing the physical labour, lessening the time required for a particular work, improving the quality of products, decreasing the human succeptibility for different diseases, decreasing pains in different injuries, fast curing from different diseases and thus, increasing the length of the human life. The life can be made quite longer. In short, the scientific and technological progress has made human life more and more luxurious.

A luxurious and longer life may not give absolute happiness to human. Absolute happiness is the important, and probably, the ultimate objective of life. The happiness is a particular state of mind.

A desire for drinking a cup of tea arises in my mind. I try to get it. My mind concentrates on preparing the tea. When I take 1st sip of tea, my desire is satisfied and I feel the happiness at that moment. I observe further that the happiness starts decreasing when I take more and more sips. The chain of the reactions can be shown as follows:

- A desire for getting something arisens in mind;
- A search for the ways satisfying the desire; and
- Concentration of mind on the ways and things desired.

- Concentration of mind on the ways and things desired

If the desire is not satisfied, there is a feeling of anger or despair	The moment at which desire, is satisfied, there is an experience of happiness
↓	↓
Erosion of values	From the next moment the happiness starts decreasing.

Firstly, one of the basic reasons for the erosion of values is the dissatisfaction of desires.

Secondly, the mind desires for hundreds of things at a time such as money, prestige, power, etc. All the desires of the mind can't be satisfied, and there will be satisfaction of some and dissatisfaction of others.

Thirdly, there is no end of desires. For example, throughout the life man eats many different things, but a time never comes in his life when he says, "I have no desire for eating". At the time of death one desires many things which are not fulfilled.

Fourthly, the mind looses its power while going through different steps — desiring for different things, searching the ways for satisfying the desires, satisfaction or dissatisfaction, etc. The mind becomes more and more feeble.

From this discussion, now, it is clear that happiness does not lie in outer things. It is the state of mind where the mind experiences the satisfaction of its desire. All the desires of the people can't be satisfied. There is no end of the desires. The mind looses its power while going through the different steps for satisfying the desires and getting happiness. If desires are not satisfied, there is a feeling of anger or despair leading to erosion of values.

Therefore, spiritualism suggests us to isolate the desire by concentrating the mind on any ideal goal or desire. It will decrease the number of desires slowly. Finally, there will be complete destruction of desires.

A scientist follows the above path. He concentrates his mind on his research. He forgets himself and tries for it until he reaches his goal. His whole life is spent in this manner. His mind concentrates on only one thing. It does not loose its power desiring for other things. As a result, he becomes powerful to discover the truth related to his research.

When a scientist attains his goal, he experiences happiness for a limited time. On the contrary, a spiritualist, after the attainment of his goal, experiences the absolute happiness and mental peace (where there is an end of all his desires). A scientist works for attaining a thing from material world. He wants to realise the laws of the nature (or *prakriti*). While a spiritualist wants to realise himself. After realising the self, there is complete destruction of desire and there is a feeling of absolute happiness.

Both the scientist and spiritualist have a single goal where they concentrate their minds. But a common man has no such single goal on which he can concentrate his mind and isolate his desire. The spiritualism, therefore, suggests him to adopt either *Rajyoga*, *Karmayoga*, *Bhaktiyoga* or *Dhyanyoga*, so that he can concentrate his mind on one thing, isolate his desire and finally escape from all the desires.

10

Science and Technological Progress

In Retrospect

S.K. Awasthi and *A.K. Singh*

Science began as man's effort to understand the nature; today, it aims at producing usable knowledge. Since science explains most of the things, even the morality has been reduced to explanation. When the problem of ethics is faced, efforts are made to solve it by research using statistics, instruments and resources rather than moral force and moral energy. The moral energy is that potential which had been displayed by Mahatma Gandhi and Abraham Lincon. This leads to promises to solve problems, which belong to the domain beyond the reach of science. Science, besides deciphering the nature, transforms it also. Technology, on the other hand, can be said to be the visible face of science, and it provides the material mediation between science and daily life. Hence, science and technology together are very well linked to development that may be expressed in terms of economic growth, industrialisation, empowerment, political participation, consumer choices, etc. In achieving our objectives, science and technology have given us all material comforts. Technology plays its role in modernising nations for fast industrialisation and ameliorating poverty in developing countries. Technology has brought material progress and higher standard of living.

Industrialisation

To achieve the mass production at faster rate, the developing countries have tried to follow and copy the economic models of developed countries and in this process, they have imported technologies from advanced western world. This means acquisition of machines, equipment, plants, process, designs, management and scientific knowledge, which is called as technology transfer.

Technology transfer, however contrary to popular belief, is not value free. Value is a "conception explicit or implicit, distinctive of an individual or characteristic of a group of those desirable traits which influence the selection from available modes and ends of action", values are the criteria for determining levels of goodness, worth, or beauty. The process of assigning or following a value system is what we go through when we evaluate or make judgment about things, events and people that we come across in our day to day life.

Technology transfer has certain inherent cultural biases and distortions which are also transferred along with it. This reflects the socio-cultural setting of the region and part of the globe where from the technology is imported. Hence, it needs to be indigenised or else it would affect the value system of the country it is exported to.

Benefit Acrued from Technology

The technological advancements to a greater extent have been able to fulfil the aspirations of the people, if not successful in minimising the perceptible gap between the rich and the poor. Through technology of the materials of daily use, infrastructural facilities, amenities, healthcare, faster transportation, communication, etc. are made available at door step of the people, to the best of their satisfaction.

The subsequent text discusses the achievements done through technology, and the impact they have made on society. The achievements have been compared and weighed *vis-a-vis* Indian culture and values.

Effect of Mass Media

Today, due to the media revolution, the rich and the poor

entertain themselves alike through television. A slum dweller is enjoying the TV serials and the song sequences the same way as a person living in sky scrappers. The other great job that the television does is of educating people on very vital requirements of human beings. All are being helped equally in the field of health, hygiene, games, sports, etc. Through application of technology, the items of daily use *i.e.*, the consumer items are being made to reach an individual according to his paying capacity. The materials in packs of different sizes from a small sachet to big sizes ranging from a kilo to a few kilos are made available to everybody. Hence, the benefits of the packaging revolution have percolated to poorer section. The credit for all this goes to the fast industrialisation through import of technology in consumer items.

The technological advancements in the field of transport sector and communication have successfully reduced distances, and the world, with the help of satellites in area of communication and Jet planes in transportation, has reduced to a global village.

But, the technological development has led the society to a situation which is in paradox to the basic nature of human being. The popularity of mass media like television has led people to 'confinement' which is against his nature, of, 'all pervading'. Due to this, the time available to a man to be socialized has reduced and this has given rise to a situation of apathy, indifference, and reduced his concern for another man. He does not find time to see whether his neighbour sleeps with full/half/empty belly or in the winter nights whether he has enough clothing to protect himself from cold.

Use of Internet

The popularity and use of 'INTERNET' and its availability have made easy access of information to everybody. Free access and easy of information to all have caused the possibility of its misuse. In our Indian culture, everybody is not supposed to possess the right to have all kinds of information. Information, for its use, is to be passed on to a 'supatra' only *i. e.*, a person who qualifies for the information. In order to become a 'supatra', one has to acquire certain skills and to be educated, and when he fulfills the requirements, he is considered fit to have and use the information. There are other evils too attached to its use like corrupting the information, hacking etc. which warrant new acts to implement the laws to curb the crime in the cyber space.

Genetic Research and Its Effects

The genetic research has provided us with comprehensive information on genetic data. The data obtained so far has already proved to be of invaluable assistance in identifying war victims, particularly dead soldiers whose bodies are mutilated beyond recognition. DNA analysis has produced foolproof results in ascertaining parentage. It has the potential to help forensic experts in pinning down the criminals, especially in serious offences like murder and rape where the criminals leave behind samples of body fluids, hair, skin or nails. These samples being like 'personal bar codes' are easily deciphered through DNA finger printing techniques.

The researchers are trying to demystify by decoding the gene responsible for hereditary diseases. The imperfect genes can be subjected to gene therapy. This genetic (Medical) information raises a possibility of use by a few companies to identify a person who may be healthy but could have a family history of particular disease and could be treated as a potential risk carrier and can be discriminated. Hence, there is a need to tread carefully between the promise held out by genetic sciences and the potential for genetic discrimination. If policy does not match advances in technology in this field, we will see an increase in number of those who have not symptoms but are treated as if they are ill "the genetic under class". Clearly, this too needs effective legislation that can protect us from misuse of genetic information and to guarantee a certain measure of genetic privacy.

The other area which the man has gained is 'cloning'. But this too poses a threat of ecological imbalance.

Education System

The education system has got a sea change as a consequence of technological progress. We had a *'Guru-Shishya'* system where it was incumbent upon a Shishya to go to a Guru's Ashram and get all kinds of training while serving the Guru. It is revealed from our ancient religious Epics like Ram Charit Manas and Ramayan that Lord Ram being son of king had to follow the tradition.

Lord Krishna too had to go the Ashram of Sandeepan Guru to learn all that was required to be known for an enlightened man. In Shrimad Bhagwad Geeta Lord Krishna while educating Arjun and readying him for the war (through his *'updesh'* in the battle field) says: that is, for learning one has to go to the Guru, sit besides him serve him, and then learn by asking questions.

But today we have a well developed modern system. Teachers coming to the house of pupil is an easy sight. We have a very well evolved system of distance learning where the education programmes are being beamed right to the house of the learner (the student). This has limited the process of learning by mutual interaction. The dimensions of the working of the brain too have been limited. The essential component of the education is the moral education, which is missing, and that is the core reason of degradation in our value system.

Need for Value Based Education

There is a basic difference between the western and Indian philosophies. We believe that the ultimate aim of a man is to have peace and happiness through satisfaction in whatever he does. Happiness really is mental and spiritual—this fact is beyond the comprehension of common man. He understands that the happiness comes from the material achievements, which are accruing through the benefits of technological advancements. Based on this notion, man joins the rat race unmindful of his ultimate aim. Without morality it is not possible to enter the depth of one's own mind. Hence, there is an urgent need for the people to be motivated towards morality to widen the experimental horizon through evolution of proper system of education. In the hands of moral people, technology would become a tool for preserving moral values rather than eroding it.

In the present age of globalization, no one could live in isolation. Religion should come together to fight the common enemy which is the hedonistic, soulless and materialistic culture spreading its tentacles all over.

Since the social and cultural milieu of the developing countries is different, they will have to make their own plan and strategy for technological progress by giving indigenous inputs. The education system will have to be built in such a way that they have their own developmental models and methodologies to achieve them. The developmental model will have to be devised in a way that it does not lead to the degeneration of the human values. The need for sharing of the information among the nations too cannot be ignored. The scientific and technological knowledge base and the human resource component of one country should be used for the benefit of the other. By this way, all will be able to make full use of technology and preserve the great Indian cultural heritage which believes in well being of everybody.

Acknowledgements

The authors gratefully acknowledge the inspiration and guidance provided by Swami Swayambodhanand in writing this paper.

11

A Compromise between Materialism and Spiritualism Through Technological Revolution

S. Padmasani Kannan

Science, technology and engineering are the most widely used words of twentieth century. These three disciplines have made impressive strides in our country during last thirty to forty years and a strong as well as wide base has been created for further repetitive technological development as well as for generation of new technology in the years to come.

Here, it is appropriate to reflect on the ultimate goal of improving conditions and standards of living of our people through the revolution brought by the above subjects. When the whole world is entering in the new millennium, the technologically advanced countries have started thinking on limits to growth and even the need for development. At this point, it behaves us well to ponder over the view on this subject of Mahatma Gandhi and his followers have talked about three levels of material achievement: squalor, sufficiency and the surfeit. While pleading for a quick transition from squalor to sufficiency, they warned us of the counter-product. Nature of the movement away from sufficiency towards forfeit from the point of view of the spiritual advancement of man conceding that the level of sufficiency may vary from one individual to another, there is need to quantify the essential needs of a human being aspiring to total advancement — physical, mental, intellectual and spiritual — in the Indian context.

The learned men of India recognised the factor of western superiority—innovations and advancement in technology and science. These advancements have brought modernisation. What do we mean by "modernisation"? Is it simply westernisation or is it simply a qualitative change among the vital institutions like family, caste, religion and society? If the latter part is our aim, how do we achieve it? To achieve this, our needs have to be analysed. It is high time that we limit the industrial growth in terms of our own culture, so that our cherished values may be cultivated assiduously and without hindrance; despite industrial progress and material advancement.

To answer this question, let us define the terms science and technology, materialism and spiritualism.

Science is the name we give to the laws that govern nature and tries to find answers to new questions and problems. How does it find? It is through the process of technology — it tries to find answers for the problems which need answers as soon as possible.

The technology in the early days was concerned with how to make fire, sharpen the stone and cultivate the land; widened the scope and exploded the knowledge in the field of manufacturing, transport, medium nuclear bombs, space research communications and so on. A child of 1999 learns more and has a wider exposure than a child of 1979. Here, the scientific and technological innovations like car, plane, transistor, television, telephone, computer, internet, fax, e-mail have brought the globe together.

A comparative study of India of 25 years before has brought a new outlook of people and the behaviour has changed. Yes — definitely a change has come — change for better or for worse. The change has culminated in structural and social transformations.

We the builders of nation are aware of the fact that these scientific advancements have brought equality. While social reformers make a much ado on these improvements, they have been continuously attacking on social customs and religion. This virulent attack has shaken the roots of our culture. Swami

Vivekananda has rightly pointed out, to cut at the roots of one nation's self-confidence would make the country to develop an inferiority complex, which is not a healthy sign. In fact, India need not be apologetic to its own culture, as it is the vitality of race. It is the neglect of spiritualism and embracing materialism completely that has brought degeneration to our country.

Wealth and prosperity are certainly needed to alleviate the poverty of the masses, but in turn acquiring wealth cannot be the aim of life. It has to give peace of mind and content. At present, we see the existence of social dualism — a society which is characterized by the co-existence of traditionalism and modernism; but unfortunately, we find strong and distinct dichotomy between traditional and modern segments with no signs of integration between the two. A close scrutiny shows that this social dualism exists because the so-called modernism is not part of the roots of the society; but is implanted on the Indian soil. This forced implantation of the society, brought through the hiatus between "materialism", and "spiritualism" is further moulded by an educational system that has aimed towards materialism and neglect of "spiritualism".

What do we mean by "materialism" and "spritualism"? It is nothing else but "*Apara Vidya*" and "*Para Vidya*" practised by our ancient system of education. While "*Apara Vidya*" talks of secular knowledge, "*Para Vidya*" talks of spiritual knowledge. While "*Apara Vidya*" imparts only knowledge, "*Para Vidya*" moulds one's character. It is the separation between the two that has brought all confusion in our system of education. Without clear mind, nothing can be observed. Swami Vivekananda has rightly pointed out how one Professor went to the laboratory but could see only a hazy picture through the microscope; the same view became clear when he cleared the spectacles and put it on the microscope. So, to view life properly, you have to keep your microscope—mind clear. Having realised the necessity of life, all great people whether it is Gandhiji or Swami Vivekananda or Socrates have emphasised on pursuing all subjects including science and technology.

At present India is among the top ten industrialised countries of the world. We are said to have the third largest body of trained scientific manpower in the world. We are the second biggest country in exporting software to the developed countries. Of course, in the beginning, our technology was based upon the researches conducted elsewhere. But the adaptive technology and the improvements made upon it have made the world turned to us. There is a great demand for our technology in many Afro-Asian and even technologically well developed countries.

Of greater concern is that the technical progress has brought a hiatus between rural and urban sectors. The highly industrialised countries of the west are concerned with pollution of the environment, depletion of mineral source needed for industry and creation of new energy. The recent data presented by an engineer shows that our air consists of 30 per cent pollution of carbon-di-oxide. There is an increase of global warming from 30°C to 60°C. A gradual rise in the sea level can be seen from 10 to 25 cm. According to the draft, Ninth Five Year Plan document, soil erosion accounts for degradation of nearly 45 per cent of the total geographical area of the country. The steady silting of the lake and the deforestation due to widening the roads or building bridges or bringing new railway lines have added to the disaster. Above all, the increasing migration of rural population to urban world has caused overflow of population in cities.

The inventions of science have played a vital role in human life. The car, the train, the plane, the photographs, the sky-scrappers, the telephone, the wireless, the e-mail, the Internet, the different types of medicines have brought a change in the living standard of the society, and have increased the life-rate. The conquest over time and space is tremendous. The technological innovations like TV, video and satellite communication systems have brought a wide awakening and equality in the society.

At present, the material concept of our present day social order has brought a morbid type of unethical outlook of modern man. Today's man's "be all and end all" has become simply to hanker after material gratifications It seems as if human beings' ultimate end in life is to struggle for the procurement of material comforts alone.

This competitiveness has decreased the ethical value of scientists and engineers. Have we succeeded in producing them with the moral commitment to society? 'No' is the answer. The technological changes have brought materialistic comfort, but it has kept a few of them alien from the society. As Dr. Nayudamma has pointed out, "the present science, technology and engineering education has produced neither the right type of manpower, nor the local problem solving capabilities".

As a result, the youth of today are challenged to cope with the competitive marketing of their potential for money and cyber comfort but they are not challenged to contribute to the quality of life on this planet. Figure 11.1 would reveal how ethical considerations, cultural affinities, scientific and technological progress and involvement in national life are interlocked. Dr. Amartya Sen, Noble laureate in Welfare Economics, has pointed out that any amount of technological explosion, change of policies and plans would be successful only if it is planned at root level. He says "there is always danger in India that you look at a good thing and you make it a bureaucratic nightmare". *The Hindu*, dated 26th September, 1999 carries an article how various development systems started in a village in Rajasthan have ended infutile. It is purely because the government does not want to involve anybody. What is felt out only is tension and blaming each other.

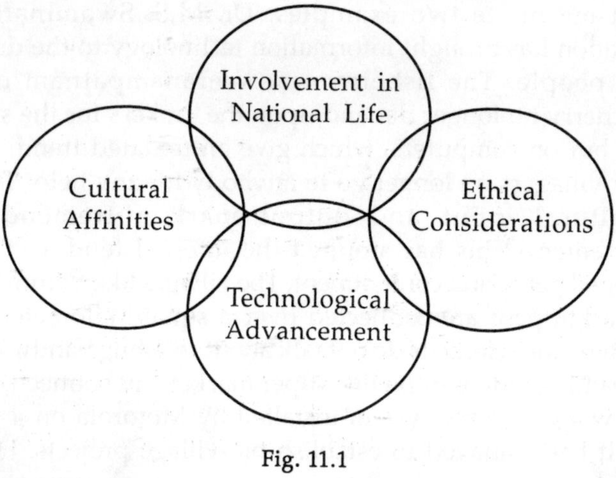

Fig. 11.1

We must remember, science and technology can bring a marvelous change in the society. Figure 11.2 shows how materialism and spritualism are interlinked when technological advancement is used for both.

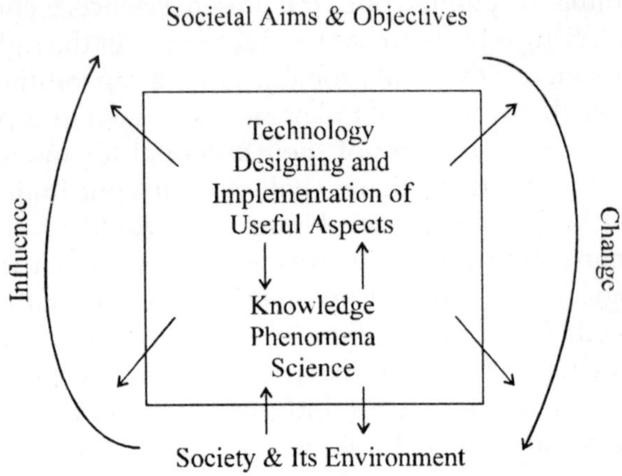

Fig. 11.1

Structural change in society and environment is brought by the influence of technology by changing societal aims and objectives.

Let me quote two examples: Dr. M.S. Swaminathan Foundation has brought information technology to the doors of the people. The fishermen at Veeranampatnam near Pondicherry no longer depend upon the brokers for the sales of fish but on computers, which give an updated trend. The Kizhur villagers no longer go to anybody for any help. Their agricultural input and output mark a tremendous improvement. This has stopped the internal feud, but has developed peace and contentment. The villages like Vilinur and Pillaiyarkuppam are connected over a square kilometers of area. Here, the scientists do not talk about swelling bandwidth, no streaming videos or on line super market, but connected by a two ways wireless system installed by Motorola on a trial basis. It has managed to establish bio-village projects. Here, the appropriate technology has been transferred. What do you mean by appropriate technology? It is nothing else but "an optimum mix of several factors—technological, economic, political, sociological and administrative. The process of this transfer includes educational process, technical seminars, information centres, intercountry industrial co-operation and free engineering".

The same has been achieved by Titan Watch Company, which is located at Hosur. The manager while presenting a case study of his company explained how the mission of this company was to employ at least a few from the local. His vision was to raise the level of the standard of life of the locals—physically, economically and spiritually. Due to this effort, the locals especially young women with basic skills combined with a little literacy are benefited. Not only they earned sufficiently, but also developed a team spirit, co-operation, concern for others. This team spirit guided them to set up their own metallic press with the help of NGOs. Naturally, the improved refinement and the cultural change had their own impact on others and slowly the alcoholism, the gambling were reduced. In short, people in and around have become sensitive to others' problems and difficulties.

One many wonder, why should Titan be struggling patiently with illiterate and disabled. This is because of the basic concepts of JRD Tata "The wealth generated by the people, needs to go back to them in the same measure or more". Maximization of profit is one of the basic concepts of any industry, but the trend is gradually changed as customer satisfaction is more important.

The technology, that has brought revolution in medicine, agriculture, education and industry, can be the tool to spread spiritualism. A video can present how marvelous changes have been brought in the lives of a village in Pondicherry, Rajasthan and Karnataka. Preservation of ancient monuments and transcriptions, renovation of architectural buildings, reading new meaning in ancient medicinal, mathematics leaflets etc. can bring a marvelous change. An Indian settled in America collects CDs on ancient epics, as he wants to pass on the experiences of the past to the new generation. Cultural continuity can be preserved. The *yoga* and meditation, in new colours, have attracted even many youngsters. The practice of this yoga is done with the background of electronic instruments. The neurologists, nephralogists and pathologists have suggested the greatness of this application.

So, technology and engineering confer a direction to the power of science and influence society deeply. Having been influenced by time and space management we must remember that our modern world is tumbling from one crisis to another. The fraudulent practices of scientific researches in Harvard University, the secretive attempt of using cloning for achieving material gains have made the scientists wonder where are we going to? Here, we should remember Dr. Kothari's mention the inhuman applications of science and the rampant violence amplified beyond imaginations, by the abuse of science and technology. We should remember the politicians and society at large are well aware of the modern world is critically dependent on technology, but they are not prepared to buy technological solutions to contemporary problems.

The scientists may be interested in abstract areas of research but it should be remembered they are the members of the society and part of an international community. Prof. Menon has rightly pointed out that as citizens of the country, the scientists have social responsibilities to ensure the applications of science, to improve the condition of our people. The best solution would be to use the science and technology to *Ahimsa*. Dr. Kothari pleaded to bring about a transition from science and technology at the expense of man to science and technology for man...".

To conclude we can say Vedanta or spiritualism advocates intense humanism. It teaches that man is the best symbol for the worship of deity. A true Vedantin can work out a programme of education, health, social uplift etc. not merely as a secular service, but as worship of God in man. Thus, the yogas of *Jnana*, *Bhakti* and *Karma* become an integrated discipline. This idea is supported by the technology policy statement that states "Indian science and technology must unlock the creative potential of people and help in building the India of our dreams".

References

Anantharaman, T.R., *Engineering and Technology — Indian perspectives.*
Anitha, D. P., *Transfer of Technology.*
Bowles, (Ed.): "Technological Innovations and Responsibilities of Scientists", Issues in Higher Education and Change.
Chittibabu, V.C.S., *Education and Social Change.*
Paul Keys, *Systems, Science and Technology in operational research system.*
Stress Gunn, *Critical issues in Information process Technology Vol I.*
Tapsyananda, Swami, *Swami Vivekananda — His Life & Legacy.*
Vivekananda, *Youth of India Arise.*
"Crime in the Lab" *The Hindu*, dated 26th June 1999.
"Learning has no Saturation Point" *The Hindu*, dated 6th Sep. 1999.
"Snatches of a Wired Rural Society" *The Hindu*, dated 6th Sep. 1999.

12

Creative Visualisation of Technology and Manifestation Through Inner Stability

Sahab Das and *Ira Das*

One of the outstanding features of the present civilisation is that the human experiences the pace of dizzy change so much that a state of uncertainty is arisen along with complexity *i.e.* 'replexity'. Hence, most of us are facing losing battle against an ocean of fresh facts that wash our consciousness steadily. To cope up with 'replexity', one requires developing a deeper level of sense of inner stability, concentration and anchor of simplicity. This can only be achieved through 'spiritualism' which, in turn, develops the deism and concentration. Of course, a certain degree of intelligence along with concentration is required to attain materialism and the advantage of technologies available for the quality of life against non-sustainable social and economical development.

It is a well-known fact that 'man' is the best creature that the God has created on this planet by giving him sufficient power and intelligence. Man can also control other creatures and utilise natural resources for his better living. At the same time, he has held him responsible for co-existence.

Hence, "Let us live and reiterate our needs for coalesce and peace out of the technological clutter".

Every one of us is haunting knowingly for one goal *i.e.* 'happiness', an invisible achievement. Hindu philosophy reveals that 'absolute happiness' is a matter beyond the world, after is the stage of conjunction of body, soul and mind. In fact, the spiritualism and the materialism go hand-in-hand by concentrating on its growth and judicious usage of technology through churning the resources. Let us not take the myopic-view of techno-economic erratic growth, and as really educated and responsible persons, our creative visualisation should be for an effective use of the available knowledge.

Technological Awareness and Involvement

"Corporates of modern India must be managed with a social conscience, else it may lead to social unrest". Mr. N.R.N. Murthi, Chairman and CEO of Infosys Technological Ltd, in the CII Seminar on 'Corporate Governance', stressed on the matter that the gap between haves and have-nots has increased so much that feudal-mindset and government restrictions at all levels have prevented the 'corporate-governance-culture' to develop. A classic example in this regard is that hybrid variety of seeds developed elsewhere were adapted to Indian conditions and soil. A proper awareness and education to users and society was as important as technology adoption, for its judiciou utilisation with minimum waste and its hazardous side effects.

The values like 'desire to do one's best' in a situation are inevitably led to conflict unless all parts and personnel movement from point to point in an identical framework of goals and timing are met. This type of co-ordination keeps the project on schedule. Flexibility *i.e.* use one's own judgement in all situation is promoted by investor usually in an established organisation which leads one to economically viable conditions. Most successful innovations are, as it is said, 'born, bred and brought to market entirely within well established organisations'. Ultimately, the above attitude and feeling that one possesses in an organisation help not only in technology diffusion but in his confidence building and in spiritual upliftment.

Case Study and Value Judgement

Real values of the society, the government and individuals should be so established that the common interests are safeguarded while adopting a new technology.

A case of 'Taj Trapezium-zone' where Agra foundries are facing the paranoia of the people due to technology transfer procedure for eliminating coke as fuel generally used in cupola furnace. It has been the result of the astute behaviour of all agencies. The Foundry Association of Agra represented that SO_2 (Sulphur Dioxide) level checked by NIRI, Nagpur had tampered the data before giving to the Supreme Court when State Pollution Board could not impress them to put scrubber. The basic idea before 1996 was to reduce SO_2 level as to minimise the acidic environment for protecting Taj Mahal from erosion. Later on, it was discovered that SPM (Solid Particulate Matter) was the culprit, not SO_2 from cupola operation. However, the proper analysis and transparency help in bringing about a new technological change, which is inevitable.

Now, to switch over from coke to gas is 'technology oriented change'. There are many changes that one has to bear, *i.e.* money oriented, time oriented, place oriented and at times, it is support oriented.

When old set of working is discarded, the man resists for the change but readily adopts even if it is costlier but easier. Whereas, the real need for the softer-approach (high quality of life) is never analysed. This disturbs the steady state of concentration. The inner stability helps bring its normal, otherwise it changes one's values and so, also, it's spiritual status. At this crucial state, one must have progressive thoughts if the change is worth adaptable. No harm, whatsoever may be the conditions forcing the change to occur. The materialistic needs require interactive thinking with retrospection, such that you control the change rather than the change controls you. The regressive thoughts have no place in the process of acclimatisation. This helps in developing a essential skill and intuitive rhythm. A certain constancy amid rising instabilities reduces stress and makes sense under replexity.

Two main functions of spiritualism work together: (i) try to rejuvenate through the practice with the 'sixth' sense which connects the soul to the super natural power (God), and (ii) morale of maintaining the body with minimum use of worldly things. This may be termed as inner stability. Two main functions of materialism are: (i) intelligent approach to the usage of facilities available, selection of life style according to the capability, and to the limit of needs, and (ii) practice to adopt a change and also, to focus on new solutions for the present needs by contemplating about the availability of technology.

A dynamic balance can be maintained, not only by the individual but also by the society as a whole to achieve absolute happiness even while living on this planet with available money, time, technology and support (resources)—with religiously following the norms set by the society to monitor the loss and the gains by the efforts made so that apparent efforts may be well directed.

It is not a querulous quid, but a reality that no regimen has been found to be suitable to govern the life style (quality of life, quantity of life, speed of life, expectations and aspirations). If a changing 'focus' of the society cannot be restricted or converged under some limits, of the man's survival, the pattern cannot be defined with any values or virtues. The new technology oriented implementations are so tempting that only (intuition rhythm, self-control and inner stability) *i.e.* 'creative visualisation' can only maintain this dynamic balance for real happiness.

Mitigation of Attainments and Values

Personality of a man differs under various circumstances and economic conditions for attaining the objectives. To be in discipline is quite tough in practice, so also at the state of defiance. Both create stress — just to achieve the best — as per social norm. Let us try to do next best and be stress free. Not all stress are bad is the conventional wisdom according to which stress increases arousal level pushing up the performances. But accumulated stress attacks at times.

Edward Dension pioneered such a study for us that technology development and attempts behind the improvement for better productivity can be treated as endogenous growth rather than exogenous growth. Even to make profit in business or to attain notable prominence in service, values like to be benevolent and virtuous in certain framework of discipline hold all good. Ultimately, the covering approach is desirable to maintain the line of 'genuflection'—flexible but creative and individualistic. Bubble like creative visualisation of our own stress is important for stable-happiness, where limits can be defined for maintaining the conjunction of body-soul-mind.

Analysis of Situation

A limit of confidence in uncertain and helpless situation is always required as first aid, which can be achieved through judicious use of technology-based supports. Even then, the faith in God's grace *i.e.* supernatural support which cannot be ignored. Advantage of the power of supernatural grace can be achieved by serving selflessly the humanity and with subdued attitude. These values can be realised, as their effects are invisible as that of materialistic gains.

Everyone visualises the problem at its own way, if animal rights are subservient to human rights, the monkeys who were released by activists from National Institute of Nutrition under experimentation for vaccine, was right or wrong? Director S.K. Basu challenges the government approach for developing technology for immunology. This will be a great set back to our scientists if such actions are encouraged in future. The scientists and engineers involved in technological enhancement cannot tolerate government interventions, which do not enhance dissemination of technical awareness.

Above all, the values of society should be analytically determined for the actions taken for the betterment of the society rather than the individuals. If, in any case, one should perceive right things in the right spirit and at the right time, the best he can do for the society.

SECTION III

HUMAN VALUES AND ENVIRONMENT

13

Human Values and Environment

M.K. Dhillon and *Gurpreet Nagi*

Introduction

Owing to scientific advancement and modernisation, women have started acquiring education at par with the men to supplement the income in order to improve the quality of life. They play a dual role both inside the houses as homemakers/ housewives and outside the home as efficient workers.

In order to maintain the balance between these two challenging jobs, they have adopted new technologies to which they value utmost for performing the speedy work both at the home and outside instead of the indigenous methods. They make use of the time and labour saving household equipments/ appliances, recreational transportation and communication devices for making the work convenient, enjoyable, interesting and most comfortable one by conserving human and non-human resources.

No doubt, these scientific technologies are the assets of human life but have some adverse effects on the individuals. They produce excessive noise which is irritating, annoying and disturbing resulting in reduced ability to work. In addition to this, people also do not attach any value to keep their surroundings neat and clean for sound mind and sound body. They are in the habit of throwing waste materials/kitchen wastes out side their homes and also not serious about open drainage system as well as stagnant water in the streets resulting in degradation of environment. A living does not apply to survival but implies to good health including physical, mental and spiritual, good quality of life to reside, work, relax and move about in a healthy environment which is free from the pollution.

Methodology

The present study was undertaken in the direction to know the sources of pollution of household and neighbouring environment on the whole. The extent of noise level was recorded from different equipments and appliances used in households whereas the traffic noise was recorded on the main roads with the help of an instrument known as Digital Sound Level Meter dB(A). The readings of noise of equipments and appliances were measured in the Equipment Lab., Department of Family Resource Management, College of Home Science, PAU Ludhiana. The equipment and appliances were categorised into different groups (Groups A, B & C) as per their workability at different speeds (Bender 1972).

In the survey, an equal number of respondents, *i.e.*, 75 each from rural and urban areas were interviewed through direct interview method. The data were collected from five villages of Ludhiana district, namely, Dakha, Lalton Kalan, Alamgir, Daad and Gahaur as well as five colonies of Ludhiana city. Fifteen respondents from each village and colony were selected randomly. In all, there were 150 respondents (housewives) from whom the data were collected. Ranking technique was administered for recording and analysing the data.

Results and Discussion

The results have been discussed with respect to sources of household and neighbouring environmental pollution and ill effects caused therefrom and amelioration of environment.

Sources of Household Pollution

These included the extent of noise produced from different equipments and appliances, fuel burning, dust through house cleaning, improper disposal of refuse, improper storage of food and water.

Table 13.1 shows that in Group A (quiet major equipments and appliances) domestic generator produced maximum noise *i.e.*, 80-85dB(A) at maximum speed followed by tape recorder/ radio respectively.

Table 13.1: Extent of Noise Levels of Household Equipment/Appliances

Name of the equipment/appliance	*Noise levels dB(A)*		
	Low Speed	*Medium Speed*	*High Speed*
Group A (Quiet major equipments and appliances)			
Television Set	-	65-67	-
Dessert Cooler	-	64	-
Tape Recorder/Radio	52	76	88
Ceiling Fan (one)	40	45	55
Refrigerator	44	-	-
Domestic Generator	-	80-85	-
Exhaust fan	-	51	-
Air Conditioner	-	61	-
Group B (Quiet equipments and small appliances)			
Electric Grinder	78	82	82
Washing Machine	-	61	-
Hair Dryer	71-72	86	86
Vacuum Cleaner	-	86-87	-
Group C (Noisy small appliances)			
Pressure Cooker	-	93	-
i) Sudden discharge of Steam	-	-	87
Thapi	60	68	71
Kundi Sota	65	68	71
Sewing Machine (Manual)	-	75-80	-

In Group B (quiet equipment and small applications), vacuum cleaner produced maximum sound [(86-87 dB(A) at medium speed] followed by hair dryer 71-72 dB(A) at low speed but 86 dB (A) both at medium and high speeds. In case of Group C (noisy small appliances) pressure cooker produced maximum noise *i.e.,* 83 dB(A) particularly when there was a discharge of steam (Table 13.1).

It is thus concluded that the noise produced from household equipments and appliances varied from 44 dB(A) to 97 dB(A) which was quite high than the acceptable noise level of 40 dB(A) prescribed by WHO.

Table 13.2 shows that among the sources of household pollution, the rural housewives gave first rank to fuel burning (3.00), followed by dust through house cleaning, improper disposal of refuse burnt material and inadequate natural light. Because of that they usually made use of wood twigs of arhar and paddy straw etc. for cooking purpose which produce excessive smoke resulting in ill health of the homemakers and other family members. On the contrary, the urban housewives gave first rank to noise from TV/radio/household equipments/ tape water/foot steps etc. as they are very much in tune for switching the communication devices at very high volume which causes nuisance to the family members as well as the neighbours.

Table 13.2: Mean ranks of miscellaneous sources household pollution in rural and urban areas

Sources	*Rural*	*Urban*
Fuel burning	3.00(I)	—
Dust through house-cleaning	3.96(II)	3.73(III)
Improper disposal of refuse	4.50(III)	3.64(II)
Ash/burnt material	5.94(IV)	—
Inadequate natural light	6.76(V)	5.25(VI)
Poor ventilation	6.97(VI)	4.13(IV)
Lack of artificial illumination	7.16(VII)	7.73(IX)
Improper storage of food & water	7.25(VIII)	6.76(VII)
Insect pests	7.81(IX)	4.34(V)
Contaminated food items	8.30(X)	7.12(VIII)
Noise from T.V./Radio/household equipment's/ foot steps/ tap water	8.61(XI)	3.01(I)

Sources of Neighbouring Environmental Pollution

Neighbouring environmental pollution included street sweepings, farm yard manure, noise from hawkers/railway line/main roads/loudspeakers and community washing at the water bodies and noise from vehicular traffic (Table 13.3 and 13.4). The first and foremost factor responsible for pollution of neighbouring environment in rural area was street sweeping (2.76). The next highest importance was attached to farm yard manure (2.94), foul smell of human wastes and burning of paddy straw which earned third and fourth ranks (3.41, 3.84) in order of their importance (Table 13.3). Along with the foul smell of human excreta as the small children had the ill-habits of easing out themselves in the streets in front of their houses or at the very outskirt of the village which were not restricted by their parents to stop this practice.

Table 13.3: Mean ranks of sources of neighbouring environmental pollution in rural and urban areas.

Rural		*Urban*	
Source of pollution	*Mean rank*	*Source of pollution*	*Mean rank*
Street sweeping	2.76(I)	Stagnant water	2.26(I)
Farm yard manure	2.94(II)	Street sweeping	2.53(II)
Foul smell of human excreta	3.41(III)	Faulty sewerage system	2.96(III)
Burning of paddy straw	3.84(IV)	Traffic noise	3.58(IV)
Faulty waste/disposal system	5.68(V)	Noise from hawkers/ railway line/ loudspeakers/building construction	4.64(V)
Noise from hawkers/ railway line, main roads/ loud speakers	6.29(VI)	Vehicular exhaust	5.63(VI)
Spraying of insecticides on fruits & vegetables	6.97(VII)	Industrial smoke	5.85(VII)
Application of chemical fertilizers in the fields	7.72(VIII)	—	—
Community washing at the bodies (well, streams, canals)	7.50(IX)	—	—

On the other hand, majority of the urban housewives expressed that stagnant water around the residential area (2.26) ranked first followed by street sweepings (2.53) and faulty sewerage system (2.96) in the form of open gutters/open drains, ranked second and third respectively in order of their importance.

Table 13.4 shows that the other important source for polluting the neighbouring environment is vehicular traffic noise.

Table 13.4: Extent of Noise Produced from the Vehicular Traffic

Name of the Sources	*Noise Levels dB(A)*	
	Average	*Maximum*
Road traffic noise	87	93
Motorcycle	78	80
Scooter	73	75
Three-wheelers	80	84
Car	71	74
Jeep	75	78
Tempo	81	76
Truck	85	92
Bus	83	86
Moped	74	82
Van	75	79

Maximum noise was produced from the trucks *i.e.*, 92 dB(A) followed by bus and tempos *i.e.* 86 dB(A). Three-wheelers moving everywhere which produced lot of smoke as well as noise *i.e.*, 84 dB(A) which lead to headache and congestion problems and irritation to ears. The acceptable noise limit should be 55 dB(A) in case of exteriors (Table 13.4).

Effects Caused by Environmental Pollution

These included air, water, noise and food pollution.

Air pollution: As regards the air pollution, both rural and urban respondents held the view that polluted air caused irritation to the eyes (Rank I) and reduced visibility which further linked with headache, nausea and dizziness. The physical ailments *viz.*, bronchitis and asthma are the results of severe air pollution through indirect inhaling of vapours of fertilizers/pesticides/chemicals used in farms and industries (Table 13.5).

Table 13.5: Mean ranks of ill-effects caused by air and water pollution in rural and urban areas

Air Pollution			*Water Pollution*		
Ill effects	*Rural*	*Urban*	*Ill effects*	*Rural*	*Urban*
Irritation to eyes	4.17(I)	3.24(I)	Sore throat	3.25(I)	3.98(III)
Suffocation	5.48(II)	5.65(VIII)	Typhoid	3.81(II)	3.88(II)
Headache	5.77(III)	4.66(II)	Dysentery	4.18(III)	4.80(IV)
Bronchitis	6.65(IV)	5.53(IV)	Cholera	4.30(IV)	5.41(V)
Asthma	6.85(VI)	5.58(VII)	Goitre formation	4.33(V)	3.48(I)
Nausea	7.34(VIII)	5.16(III)	Tonsils	6.49(VI)	5.66(VII)
Reduced workability due to dizziness	8.18(X)	6.62(IX)	Hepatitis	7.69(VIII)	5.54(VI)
Soiliness of clothes and household articles	7.85(IX)	7.38(X)	Inbreeding of mosquitoes and flies	7.12(VII)	7.01(VIII)
Destruction of white wash exterior paint	6.66(V)	5.34(IV)	Destruction of field crops	8.22(IX)	8.48(IX)
Destruction of vegetation	7.12(VII)	5.44(V)	Destruction of fisheries	10.00(X)	10.00(X)
r (ranks) = 0.82*			r (ranks) = 0.83*		

* *Significant at p = 0.01.*

Besides this, they also suffered from suffocation during harvesting wheat and paddy due to dusty atmosphere during that time.

Water pollution: As regards the water pollution, respondents from the categories complained sore throat, tonsils, dysentery, cholera and typhoid etc. (Table 13.5).

Noise pollution: In this context both rural and urban respondents expressed irritation to ears followed by headache, disturbed sleep, reduced working efficiency, rise in blood pressure and restlessness (Table 13.6).

Table 13.6: Mean Ranks of ill effects caused by noise pollution and unhygienic food rural and urban areas.

Noise Pollution			*Unhygienic Food*		
Ill Effects	*Rural*	*Urban*	*Ill Effects*	*Rural*	*Urban*
Irritation to ears	2.06(I)	2.52(I)	Stomachache	2.30(I)	2.03(I)
Headache	2.74(II)	2.53(II)	Food poisoning	2.80(II)	2.93(II)
Annoyance	4.86(V)	3.90(IV)	Dysentery	3.70(III)	4.00(IV)
Disturbed sleep	4.46(IV)	3.74(VII)	Nausea	4.01(IV)	3.25(III)
Reduced working efficiency	4.16(V)	4.34(V)	Vomiting	4.33(V)	4.21(VI)
Rise in blood pressure	6.53(VII)	6.49(VII)	Cholera	5.34(VI)	4.54(VII)
Restlessness	4.58(VI)	4.97(VI)	Gastric ulcers	6.00(VII)	4.18(V)
r(ranks)=0.82*			r(ranks)=0.85**		

* *Significant at p = 0.05.* ** *Significant at p = 0.01.*

Food pollution: Stomachache (Rank I) and food poisoning (Rank II) were reported to be the most common symptoms occurring among the rural and urban inhabitants (Table 13.6). They also suffered from other ill effects like nausea, dysentery, diarrohea, vomiting and gastric ulcers etc. by using stale food, improper ways of cooking food in the open kitchens, without wiremesh doors and windows (Table 13.6) resulting into unhygienic conditions.

Amelioration of Environment

It referred to the improvements to be made in the household as well as the neighbouring environment. The rural housewives gave their priorities to the use of biogas, LPG, installation of smokeless *chullha*, use of dried fuel which can help avoiding smoke drudgery and ultimately avoiding air pollution (Table 13.7). They also expressed that there should be well-equipped kitchens having the provisions of exhaust fans and chimneys along with water facilities, use of garbage bins which contribute towards obtaining healthier environment.

As regards the amelioration of neighbouring environment, both rural and urban respondents held the view that there should be more of T.V. coverage concerning the environmental amelioration as it is usually possessed by rich/poor people either black and white or coloured as a source of recreation which can also prove educative in such programmes (Table 13.7). The respondents also expressed that there should be tree plantation on roadsides which could help to purify the air to make the environment free from the air pollution.

Table 13.7: Mean ranks of priority of respondents regarding factors for the improvement of households as well as neighbouring environment in rural and urban areas.

Household Environment			*Neighbouring Environment*		
Factors	*Rural*	*Urban*	*Factors*	*Rural*	*Urban*
Use of LPG (gas chullah) biogas	2.97 (I)	3.25 (I)	Tree plantation on road side	3.17 (I)	2.96 (III)
Installation of smokeless chullah	6.78 (VII)	10.50 (XI)	TV & Radio programmes	3.49 (II)	2.26 (II)
Use of dried fuel	3.58 (VI)	4.88 (III)	Covered wells	4.18 (III)	9.12 (XI)
Water facilities along with proper waste disposal system	5.81 (IV)	6.62 (VIII)	Institution/ non-institution short training courses	7.93 (VIII)	7.05 (VI)
In-built kitchen with urlemesh door	5.88 (V)	4.48 (II)	Municipality efforts (proper placement of garbage, cleaning the drains)	10.00 (X)	2.14 (I)
Wiremesh doors/ windows in the house	6.17 (VI)	6.46 (VII)	Improve quality of diesel	6.92 (VII)	6.28 (V)
Use the garbage bins/pits	5.70 (III)	4.90 (IV)			
Commercial spray to male the house insect free	7.88 (XI)	6.80 (X)	Environmental education (courses on environment in school & college curriculum)	6.00 (IV)	7.20 (VII)
Use of exhaust fans/chimneys	7.10 (VIII)	6.80 (IX)	Governmental efforts (law, rules, acts)	6.30 (V)	4.13 (IV)
Hygienic storage	7.53 (IX)	5.48 (VI)	Voluntary organisations	8.24 (IX)	7.37 (VIII)
Miscellaneous (adequate natural light, artificial lighting, regular white wash, proper flooring etc.)	7.54 (X)	—	Miscellaneous (proper use of resources like water, oil, fuel, etc. Proper placement of household wastes, celebration of van-mahotsav etc.)	6.25 (VI)	7.74 (IX)

Conclusion

People should be aware of the environmental degradation which ultimately affects the development of sound mind and sound body. There is a universal instinct in man to enjoy a comfortable living through judicious use and proper exploitation of limited resources at his/her hand. Women can also create such an environment in her home which is free from pollution, particularly air, water, food and noise pollution, ultimately resulting into contented life. Man must learn to control population size and develop more efficient technologies that produce as little harmful wastes as possible. Still, we are long away from becoming a sustainable-oriented development society.

Reference

Bender, E.K. (1972), "Noise from Construction, Home Appliance and Building Equipment", *J. ENVIRON., SCI.*, Sept./Oct., 9-18.

14

Man-nature Relationship and Human Values

Sudhira Chandra Jena

Man's endeavour to evolve a mutually re-enforcing relationship with nature is age old. Man has maintained this relationship for which life on planet earth has survived. Had there been any deviation in this relationship, life would have disappeared long ago. Man evolved values which helped him co-exist with other forms of life and with nature as a whole. The sources of such values are intuitive and experiential knowledge of several years. In fact, much of what we call culture is the sum total of these values and the behaviour patterns emanating from them.

I

Man-nature Relationship

We see man-nature relationship in primitive period of history. In our epics we see close relationship between man and nature also. Rama Chandra, (the hero) of *"Ramayan"*, spent 14 years in jungle. Lord Krishna spent his childhood in *'Kunja Bana'* (the garden or natural forest by the side of river Yamuna). The young boy Dhruva came in contact with Lord in deep forest. Buddha got salvation under the tree 'Bodhidruma'. Parvati, the daughter of Himalaya, adopted penance in summer, rain and winter in forest to have Shiva. In the present day, people in rural areas plant peepal and banyan trees mostly at roadsides and afterwards, they make them marry as a token of Aryan culture. There are instances, people marry 'Sahada' tree when their wives die in a regular interval. People worship 'neem' tree as a token of respect to Lord Jagannatha as the 'begraha' is made of neem woods. Similarly, on the occasion of *Shakti Puja* people worship 'Bael' tree. With the first drop of rain on earth, people of Orissa observe 'Raja' festival to worship Mother Earth (not to dig, not to put fire on earth etc.).

II

So long as the society was simple and essentially agricultural, the traditions set by the value system offered enough scope for man to meet his basic needs while working within the limits set by the nature. Any transgression of these limits was temporary, localized and often unintentional. And hence, it did not take much time for the balance to be restored.

Industrial revolution changed man-nature interaction. One can trace the roots of this worldview to earlier philosophies and thoughts of Greeks. Rene Descartes and Newton are the father figures of this new paradigm. Adam Smith extended it to economics.

This paradigm abandoned the age old man-nature eco interaction and gave rise to a new thought process and belief that nature is a resource and is meant to be exploited by man to improve his material well being. Man, being the supreme creation of God, has the privilege as well as the right to use nature the way he deems fit. Here comes the crisis of ecological and environmental problems. Nature has been overused. Man has not only broken the laws of nature but also tried to change them. And each time man took a major step to overreach nature, he got nature's retribution in the forms of disasters and miseries. That man is paradox of extremes has been uncovered in the closing decades of 20th century. Man possesses untold knowledge of wealth but has not brought universal end to the human indignity, poverty and ignorance. His mastery of science and technology has given him unprecedented power but has the humiliation of making his own world a slum. Old values and established practices are being challenged all over the world. The advocates of environment and ecology suspect man as an unintelligent, inefficient and irrational animal because they believe that human knowledge and modern science and technology would come to the aid of man. The symptoms of the problem of ecology and environment are misunderstood as the causes. The remedial measures are, therefore, temporary and often counter - productive. A solution of one problem gives rise to more and newer problems. We have to realise that science and technology are only tools or measures to achieve something but not sustainable.

III

Value Change

Value is not fixed for ever. But in the context of environment, human values are: (a) Means Values, and (b) End Values.

Means Values

Means values are called process values or instrumental values which help in maintaining a good relationship between man and nature.

Examples of these values are love and generosity. Love includes the love for animals, plants and fellow human beings, helping the distressed, old and helpless, sharing the feeling of others, and forgiveness. Voluntary action for mutual help, pleasure in helping others, politeness, kindness, compassion and sacrifice are the other forms of values.

End Values

End values are final values of human life. These help us move towards the state of existence. The examples of end values are peace, tranquility, security, equality, fraternity, freedom, wisdom, inner harmony, non-exploitation, a balanced global system and an egalitarian world order. Here the planet earth is one family. We should work for all. Exist and let others exist is the *'mantra'*. Here there is no scope for personal pleasure. Greatest happiness of the greatest degree is the basic principle. We consider what we have given or done to this planet not what we have received. Spiritual development is the ultimate value, because material development has no boundary. It is endless. It kills the real happiness of life. It develops anxiety and invites problem which kills the vitality of human life.

In nutshell, we can say that love for earth, ecologically positive behaviour, compassion towards all living things and sharing of earth's resources with limitations to our greed will bring a world of beauty a balanced global ecosystem and green economics where there will be proper rainfall, monsoon, no drought, no cyclone, no earthquake and a balanced society, where we can fill our needs.

These values impose certain limitations on human conduct with regard to the nature. Sometimes these limitations are voluntary and sometimes obligatory and their violation incurs punishment.

IV

Human Values and Environment

Human values with regard to environment has different dimensions. The protection and conservation of the nature are important because they are for the interest of the man. In Indian philosophy, the whole world is considered to be one family. The living as well as non-living elements on the earth are interdependent and difficult to separate them. Since the survival of man depends on the natural environment and since the nature provides the means of livelihood, man should use the nature judiciously.

Before the advent of industrial revolution, the pressure of population was light, the production and consumption was unseparated, the man's requirements were limited to the basic needs of food, clothing, housing, education, security and self-esteem, and production was localised and on small scale.

Industrial revolution brought a sea change in the pattern of life and living of human being. Modern science and technology, industrialisation, urbanisation, mass production and divorce of production from consumption put a lot of impact on the human life and on the environment also. Environmental pollution, mass poverty, over population and consumerism dominated the scene. When the rich exploited the natural resources for their purpose, the poor had to takeout their living from natural resources. The result is the wanton destruction of the nature by the rich and the poor alike, which ultimately is the living threat of climatic change, depletion of ozone layer, and pollution of land, water, air and vegetation.

To protect our environment and eco-system, we have made laws. UN, national governments as well as judicial bodies have made new laws and strengthened the old ones. But till date we have not been successful in achieving the target.

V

Conslusion

To maintain a sound relationship between man and nature, emphasis should be laid on education. Values of parents are transmitted to their children. Besides formal schooling, family members, relatives and neighbours are other educators for the children. Present day formal schools are the products of the industrial society. Even the Third World countries have the same education system. Children have been taught to treat nature as material resources; as a means to the end; not the end itself. Reorientation of our formal educational system towards value-based learning and teaching is essential and urgent in order to halt the drift we notice today.

So far the relation between the man and the environment has been looked at mainly from the standpoint of the man. It is time now to consider the other side, by looking at environment itself on a world scale. It has now become inevitable that man should not only manage the nature but should also learn to manage himself as part of the nature.

The old structures of law and institutions would in no way respond to the pathetic plight in which mankind has plunged by its own work. A new legal institution has to emerge to combat and control the situation.

Finally, governmental institutions, non-governmental organisations, people, educational institutions, political parties, decision makers as well as administrators should take vow to make aware the people to have a permanent human value towards environment for sustainable development. Emphasis should be given on spiritualism of Eastern culture.

References

Mishra, R.P. (1995), "Environmental Ethics and Jurisdiction Relationships and Interdependence" in *The Indian Journal of Public Administration*, Vol. XLI, No. 3, pp. 555-62.

Nagaraja, H.K., *Environmental Revolution — A Management Crisis.*

Strong, Maurice F. (1972), "The UN and the Environment" in *International Organisation*, Vol. 26, p. 169.

15

Human Values and Environment

Shraddha Shukla

Introduction

In the present age of aggressive rationality, rapid materialism and excessive faithlessness, human values are losing weight. Pollution is deeply rooted in one's living and way of thinking and is continued to be socio-cultural crisis that has badly affected the total environment. There is a wide gap between what is being produced and what is needed by the society. Now-a-days, happiness lies in material success, and the human values of morality, honesty, dutyfulness, mutual co-operation, commitment for human welfare and humanity remain unhonoured. The devaluation of moral values is no more an individual's problem, but it is a social problem. It has assumed global proportions, so there is an urgent need of morality that should become an integral part of everybody's personality.

In the era of science and technology, science is working as the most iconoclast of established traditions and values. The ailments of present society can be cured to a great extent through the provision of an effective, meaningful and value-based learning. Education is not treated as part and partial of the human environment and has almost ceased to function as a vital human factor. Environment is a set of relationships between man and nature, and the environmental disequilibrium is the product of neglectful activities of human being. The question arises what makes a person to pollute the environment? Whether he does it consciously or unconsciously?

The psychological micro environment of a person is so minute that he is unable to see beyond his own interest. Unfortunately, he visualises the interests which are countable in terms of money. "The central purpose of human life is to maximise one's effectiveness as a competitor and to merge one's individuality with the system". If we look at this system from a distance, it becomes clear that its dominant values are self-centredness and greed.

Duality in Man's Nature

The fast growing industriali-sation leading to urbanisation and, finally, creating a materialistic attitude among the people has developed such an alarming situation that 82 per cent of the population has to depend upon only 15 per cent of its resources. So-called 'modernisation' is the iconoclastic behaviour of technology. Technological progress has distorted the basic culture as per needs of the human being. The question arises that why a person is after the false paradise leaving the realistic approach of life? To solve this question one has to consider psychological and philosophical approaches.

In order to fast building empire, man is cutting down forests, diverting waters to generate power and harnessing natural energies for his own interests. Industrialisation, modernisation and globalisation, on the one hand, and socialisation, social transformation and social integration, on the other, are the outcome of man's labour. However, all these are meant for physical maturity, but the man can realise that civilisation is not a mere product of physical maturity or material satisfaction. He is the medium in the sense that all his energies are meant to promote him. The noetic character of man is always high above the phenomenal attribute, perhaps to receive the new messages of the universal selfconsciousness. Thus, in common observations, we find a duality in man's nature. He is not 'self-creative', nor 'self-inspiring' in his action. He gets more satisfaction in 'detachments' than in his 'attachments'. The pleasure of unseen is more real than that of the seen. He has many folds and multidimensions in his nature.

What is Value

In spite of a man's greatness and richness, the most unfortunate is that he is not happy because of his 'fragmentation' or 'disintegration' of diverse qualities *'rajoguna'*, *'tamoguna'* and *'satoguna'* which are often concealed, while technology tends to create properties that revealed through action. Qualities are generic and concealed, whereas properties are static and revealed through action. When a quality tends to fulfil a human need or evoke feeling of pleasure, it creates 'value'. This is purily a subjective concept. It differs from situation to situation and even from individual to individual. Still, there are certain absolute values like truth, honesty, sense of duty and responsibilities which hold in all ages and in all places. Technological advancement has distorted these absolute values.

Values have no spiritual basis, but they spring from the given environment and are considered as total modes of human behaviour i.e. physical, vital, mental, psychic, economic and spiritual. They interpenetrate one another and influence a social change in a given environment. The whole universe (or *brahmanda*) is the expression of physical values or reality of *'panch-tatva' i.e.* in form of earth, air, water, ether and fire. Psychic values are higher values rooted in volitional nature of individual in the form of thinking, feeling and willing; while economic values are common observations that are convertible or exchangeable.

Values *vis-à-vis* Environment

In contemporary society, absolute values and intrinsic values are losing their weight, and social, political and economic values based on social stratification are gaining. The organisation of these different values shape the environment. An imbalance in *Rajoguna*, *Tamoguna* and *Satoguna* causes distortion in man's personality in the form of 'ego', *'Aaham'* and 'thirst', *'Trishna'*. Man's activities become more and more physical in order to fulfil endless *'Trishna'*. More and more materistic attitude in human leads him to more and more exploitation of the nature.

So there is an urgent need to balance the nature of qualities of *Rajoguna*, *Tamoguna* and *Satoguna*.

In fact, man has broken his links with the nature and is trying to establish his own independent empire of thought in the realm of consciousness. He is out to organise and re-organise the nature inviting a wide gulf between him and the nature. He has tamed the nature, and now, is trying to improve it as to become a superman. Real perfection to a man needs his faith in God, sincerity, aspiration to humanity and devotion to duty, but he behaves otherwise. He thinks that knowledge is limited and all truths are at his disposal. That ultimately causes all sorts of distortion of human values in which technological progress creates a field.

Conclusion

At the end, I would like to exhort that there is a high mounting demand for an ideal educational system based on the philosophy of optimum development of three basic faculties —heart, head and hand *i.e.*, in the form of '*Vidya*', '*Vivek*' and '*Kaushal*'. There should be a harmonious blend of science and spirituality, intellect and intuition, analysis and synthesis. For that, the whole system should be knowledge-based, value-based and need to satisfy human intrinsic and extrinsic nature as a totality.

References

Jack L. Nelson, *Redical Ideas and the School*, Renehard and Winston Inc., New York.

Jawaharlal Nehru, *The Emerging World*, Asia Publishing House, Volume I.

16

Dangers to Human Values and Environment Due to the Development of Modern Science

A. Balasubramanian

Economy, environment and human values are interdependent and interfolded. Human values were given more importance by Gandhiji, Bharathi and Bharathidasan. The famous Tamil poet, Bharathi said, "If there is no food for one person, we should completely destroy the whole world". Bharathidasan said, "We will create a brave new world". Now, there is a will for the Ghandhian economics as it is based on the *Swadeshi* policies. Both the IMF and the World Bank had asked India to follow Argentina, Indonesia, Brazil, Malaysia, Korea etc. But all these countries are struggling too much of economic recessions and they face great economic problems. These agencies kept mum, and now, they are suggesting us to follow globalisation. A true global economy could not emerge until all currencies are united and backed by a single global reserve of foreign exchange.

Globalisation is a creation of the developed countries. Wall Street Journal has said that India should be followed by all countries to save their countries from the above world economic recessions.

Vivekananda said, "We are going to live for a short period. During that period we must live with more enjoyment and statelihood and not as water bubbles which come and go". Modern human economists suggest globalisation as the solution for all problems. But New Week has said that "Globalisation based on capitalism is a failure". Soros believes that the modern IMF and World Bank are themselves facing problems and they could not suggest solutions to the world countries regarding environment and human development.

Developing countries' money is swallowed by the monopolistic developed countries like HIV AIDS virus which swallows all RBCS. The developing countries do not have money to invest in the environmental projects.

Tagore has said that "The God has created different kinds of questions to different countries. No country should follow the other country's policies". Nuclear energy is the milestone of the modern science's discovery. We have already faced the Chernobyl nuclear disaster. We have faced the three mile nuclear plant disaster in the USA. It has been estimated that the oil resources in India will come to an end within 13 years and before 2040, all the earths' resources will change places.

Science can denature plutonium. But we cannot denature evil in the heart of the man, says Einstein. Shakespeare said, "There is a very silent line between the harshness and the peacefulness of the God. But nobody cares for it". The Bible says that the world will face a boggy experiment which is waiting during his period (*yuga*) and we have a fight very hard to overcome it. Max Muller had said that "whatever sphere of human mind you may select for your special study, you have to go to India". According to *Agama Sastra*, the world is real and not an illusion.

God made this land, sky and sea. But his best creation is man. Man's best creation is modern science.

Nehru said, "India needs a new industrial and human revolution which could only save the State's investment and pave way for industrial and individual development". These things can now be possible only through computer technological revolution.

Today, the computer science has given us the ability to create life out of test tubes. Dr. Raman said that the "Theories of sciences were not ultimate facts of reality but only temporary statement of ideas". Our ancients, who laid stress on science, thought that it was not ultimate facts of reality but only temporary statement of ideas that helped people. They stressed both on science (adi boutika) as well as spirituality (adhyatmika) but put more importance on spirituality. Adi Sankaracharya stated that "a doctrine that fails to save the life disappears or has no validity". Dr. Raman said "the Indian methods were speculative and synthetic but the western approach as analytical, discursive and separatist. Modern science and technology are only considered as tools for finding out the problems and helping people to solve their problems". But science has to go for the desire for the fruits of action, realisation of tranquility, cultivation of self restraints, renunciation, patience and peace of mind (*shamadamadi sampat*) and the desire for spiritual liberation and salvation of human problems. Dr. Raman said, "Modern scientific truths might appear to be valid in their own limited physical sphere but they had no relevance to other dimensions of existence and reality". Ancient sages were great scientists and their works were used for the public welfare. Even, Vysa had anticipated before Einstein with regard to the theory of relativity. Ancient people believed that man was a part of the cosmos and there was a link between the macrocom (the cosmos) and the microcosm (man) *e.g.* solar flares and cardio vascular troubles, the moon's movements and mental aberration, the sun-spots and economic cycles, etc.

Astrology is a vast subject with 4 lakh sutras, which should be analysed and followed. These sutras were coined by ancients based on intuitive observations and experiments. We must immediately look for the tentacles of modern science in other fields of study like the precious stones and their connection with Astrology, healing of diseases, and framing the future. Chesterfield said, "No idleness, no laziness, no procrastination, never put off till tomorrow what you can do today". Much of the world's problems could be solved by modern technology but it must be based on moral, physical and spiritual values. So only the IBM symbol is "I don't want to think about the future but I want to own it".

A poet has said that "your knowledge must glitter all over

the universe and all the living things in the whole world must enjoy through it". So science should help people to solve their problems. People must think of these things. The research has to be directed more towards human problems' solving. The technology/modern science should help the people to get more businesses through natural resources. The availability of key raw materials, electricity and cheap labour will doubtlessly lead us to a vigorous and multi-dimensional growth of our industries. We should make available scientific information to those who use them for our national development.

Computer and information technologies will help us foster formal links with various business agencies all over the world, and we can identify the tasks and solution of problems. According to London press service, "Due to modern technology, a big change has happened and the science development has given ways to a realistic commitment to today's problems". National Policy on Education described that "Designing and implementing research programmes relevant to the changing requirements are not under taken on a wide enough scale".

Mahatma Gandhi said that "the strength of a chain was in its weakest link. So, if a section of scientific people is considered to be weak, then the strength of the whole nation is affected". We do not want to use our expertise fully but we are looking at other countries for proven technology. Tiruvalluvar has said that "the value of help rendered by science to the people is not based on the value attached to it but depends on the value of one who receives it". We should boldly seize what is new, examine the opportunities and adopt what suits us.

The computer revolution has already overtaken the world. It is an invisible army that has changed the world's way of life and work. The computer has changed the whole business world and has brought an impersonal culture among people. The world is even now frightening about the Y2K problem.

Scientific studies are to be improved in finding out the reasons for the formation of earthquakes, storms etc., nuclear bombs and leakings are considered to be the dangerous things now-a-days. Edmund Falt Ermanyer suggests that new and safer design for nuclear power plants should be framed to alleviate the green house effects. Charistopher Flavin argues that renewable energy sources, not nuclear power, are the more sensible alternatives. Buckmister Fillker has said, "Spaceship earth must be saved by everybody". Forests have gotten smaller each year, the deserts have gotten larger. The top soils have gotten thinner.

The ozone layer is apparently being deplored. The atmospheric carbon-di-oxide levels are rising, biological diversity is diminishing. Toxic wastes are accumulating.

Scientific developmental policies that are not grounded in an environmental context are failing now-a-days. Success is possible only if we formulate the ecologically sustainable development strategy. Companies that build nuclear power reactors should work on new models which are very safer to the environment. A switch from coal or oil to other fuels is necessary. Coir pith blocks can be used as alternative to coal. More funding should be given for solar, wind, renewable and geothermal power plants and projects. Protection to ozone layer is the need of the hour. More emission of CO_2 from fossil burning causes damage to the ozone layer and environment. Climate check is a terrible thing to be discussed as global temperature is increasing by few degrees.

Warming of earth will result in rising of sea levels due to ice changing into water. The hot climate will increase 12 times. Rise in sea level will result in engulfing of more islands. Many of the islands which are only a few metres above sea level, may go into water. The accord of 1987 calls for the world countries to reduce or eradicate the manufacture of CFCS: Chloroflouro carbons by the end of the century. The World Bank now-a-days go for financing firewood projects.

Vedas are considered as a weapon to contain the process of free discussion that took place between human beings over thousands of years. It contains the principles of our old tradition and free thinking. The *Gita* is a system of specification as well as a rule of life, an intellectual search for truth, as well as an attempt to make the truth dynamic for achieving the goal of man. *Gita* speaks of the solutions to the human beings for their restlessness, impossible aspirations, unending desires, utter disillusionments, suffocation despairs, entombing dejections, the shattering confusion, etc. Nanak has said that God is in your body, in your office, in your factory, in your home, and in the bazzar.

17

Environmental Pollution Attributable to Technology Transfer to Immoral Persons

Experience from Primary Sector

K.M. Mohapatra

Introduction

Today, human realises that environment and eco-system are important common properties for his survival and sustainable development. These properties are governed by the nature. Their preservation has become the fundamental duty of the human being. Technological invention is the knowhow about the nature brought to human use. In that sense, the nature and technological inventions are interrelated. Again, the human being is a part of the nature. Thus, technology, human and the nature are interdependent. The development will be sustainable if a congenial relation to each one is maintained among them. In many instances, invention of technical knowhow in a particular field is mainly based on human needs. When a human feels any sort of discomfort in his living, he searches out a solution in technical form. Necessity is the mother of invention. From this angle, objective of an invention of technology is not to disturb or dismantle the nature and environment. In course of time, misuse and mismanagement of a technology are started when human value consideration is detached from it. This happens with those people who change their mentality towards selfishness and shortsightedness for some materialistic achievements. A technology transfer to unscrupulous persons may lead its misuse and mismanagement. Under such circumstances, the environment and human welfare are affected because of adversity of technology. Again, in some cases, the technological inventions are designed in order to serve the evil desires of some unscrupulous persons. Invention of electronic virus to damage software in computer is one of such examples. These types of technological inventions are highly dangerous to the human and its environment. However, any technological invention whether it is human-need based or based on evil desires, if it lacks conformity with human value system, it may be, sooner or later, proved to be harmful to the mankind and the environment.

Technological inventions in several fields of human requirement gave birth to industrial revolution and green revolution and, recently, to cybernetic revolution. Consequently, industrialisation and urbanisation took an exponential growth trend all over the world. Human could able to meet most of its desires for necessaries, comfortables and luxuries. Gradually, money, wealth and power became the central part of human desires. Every society in the world tried to have quick growth in these three things. Economically better-off nations tried to become further more powerful and started to show their economic supremacy. In these lines, competitions of rich vs rich, producers *vs* producers and consumcers *vs* consumers were started for the sake of more money, more wealth and more power. Technology was moulded accordingly to meet such competitive environment. That led to mass production and mass consumption, which was made possible through over-exploitation of natural and human resources with the help of technology and science. At each stage of development, human values were neglected.

In this essay, an attempt is made to study the relationship between technology, human values and environment, in the development of primary sector of the economy. The study highlights the following issues: how did technological progress in agriculture, mining, quarrying and fishing lead towards overexploitation of natural resources, and consequently, to environmental pollution and ecological imbalance? How is technology transfer to unscrupulous and immoral persons responsible for its misuse and mismanagement? How human value consideration is missed in technological and scientific application? and how does WTO patent policy on life-form technologies have implications of violation of human and socio-cultural value norms? This essay contains five sections including introductory part. The study is based on both primary and secondary information.

Agrochemical Technology, Capitalist Farmers and Environmental Issues

The agrochemical technology comprises of chemical fertilizers, chemical pesticides and additives used in agriculture and agricultural preservation. This is considered an important part of green revolution technology. Since 1960, the world has achieved a tremendous increase in food production, and subsequently, the impact of global food scarcity has been lessened. Many countries which, were perennially prone to food-scarcity and human hunger in the past, have become self-sufficient in food. Of course, this is a great economic success, which is largely attributable to chemical and HYVs technologies in agriculture. Later on, towards late 1970s and onwards, many green revolution belts in developed economies faced environmental problems mainly originating from agro-chemicals and overexploitation of land and water resources. Excessive application of agrochemicals to fixed arable land by farmers caused environmental and ecological problems like air pollution, water eutrophication, groundwater depletion, loss of bio-diveristy, land degradation, toxicity of agricultural products and so on.

At the global level, a large quantity of fossil fuel is required for cultivation, irrigation and manufacturing fertilizers and pesticides. Agricultural use of fossil fuel has increased about six-to-eight fold since 1950. It now takes twice as much oil to produce a ton of grain as it did 40 years ago (Jerry, *et al.* 2000).

The proportion of carbon di-oxide and other pollutants emanating from the agricultural use of fossil fuel and from the disposed massive farm waste has significantly increased over last few years. Such addition to air pollution and ozone layer damage has now become a matter of great concern (Gaur: 1997 and Montreal Convention on CFC: 2000).

For a spectacular achievement in raising agricultural production and becoming self-dependent in food, India is highly obliged to agrochemical and HYVs technologies. Since early 1950s, the country has witnessed a geometrical growth in the application of agrochemicals to its agriculture. The use of chemical fertilizers (NPK) in agriculture, which was only 66.7 thousand tonnes in 1951-52, increased to 13.54 million tonnes in 1994-95 (Majumdar: 1994 and Dahiya: 1996). The amount of chemical pesticides used in agriculture was merely 1,000 tonnes in 1950-51, and that had increased to 83,000 tonnes in 1994-95 (Dahiya: 1996). The average use of pesticides per hectare cropped area increased from 3.2 gms in 1954-55 to 454.0 gms in 1993-94 (Gracy: 1996). Between 1966 and 1995, the agricultural use of chemical fertilizers and pesticides was increased ten times. The index of agricultural outputs increased from 46.0 in 1950-51 to 169.2 in 1996-97 (1980-81 being 100). The per capita foodgrain availability (domestically) was 0.379 kg per day in 1951 which increased to 0.561 kg per day in 1996 (Sengupta: 2001).

No doubt, in Indian economy, the chemical technology played key role in the development of agricultural sector. But the blessing of such technology on the economy was at the cost of environmental safety, ecological balance and socio-cultural ethos. In many agriculturally developed regions, the chemical technology has caused environmental hazards in different manners.

Surface and ground water pollution is largely attributable to excessive application of chemical fertilizers and pesticides in agriculture. According to a study, about 70 per cent of all the available surface water in India is polluted (Karpagam: 1991). The agricultural sector is considered to be the main source of water pollution, particularly in green revolution areas. The chemical fertilizers applied to land are partly absorbed there and partly flown to water bodies through water run-off. Land absorbs fertilizers up to its limit, and beyond that, it lets to water run-off. Its excessive use means excessive supply to water bodies. Excessive deposits of nutrients (fertilizers) in water bodies help algae and large aquatic plants to wildly grow there. The process of nutrition supply to algae and weeds in water is called eutrophication. Due to eutrophication in any water body such as in rivers, ponds, lakes and seas, the BOD (Biological Oxygen Demand) level increases which indicates a higher degree of pollution, and consequently, aquatic lives find difficulty to survive there. Similarly, pesticides in soil are carried into ponds, rivers, lakes and seas by run-off water in dissolved or in soil particle forms. Once the lethal pesticides contaminate water, it accounts for a massive damage of aquatic lives. One of the major harmful effects of the use of pesticides is on the regenerative function of the ecosystem (Jindal and Singh: 1989). The insecticides have been causing particular concern with regard to their residual toxicity in human body.

A survey report of the Central Plant Protection Training Institute, Hyderabad (1984) revealed that in Ludhiana (an agriculturally developed region) there were various fruits, vegetables and grains which were containing pesticide residues above the permissible level. The consumers face health hazard through a low level exposure to pesticides by consuming pesticides contaminated foods. According to a report of National Academy of Sciences (USA) in 1987, about 20,000 cases of cancer were caused by the pesticides in food (Jerry, *et al.* 2000).

Pesticides usually kill off most of the pests' natural predators and many micro-organisms those generally considered beneficial to farmers directly or indirectly. Again, in tropical regions, insects and pests became resistant to specific pesticides in less than 3 years. In order to fight against it, improvement in quality and doses of pesticides were required which became highly hazardous to the environment and eco-system [Miller: 1990].

Both chemical fertilizers and pesticides damage bio-diversity (Mohapatra: 2001). There are also instances of ground water pollution, particularly in green revolution areas, due to excessive application of nitrogen to land. Nitrogen can enter the ground level beyond the root zone of the most crops (Venkateswarlu: 1985).

Excessive use and mismanagement of chemical inputs in agriculture are found in the agriculturally developed regions. In these regions, over past years, a group of farmers has emerged from the agrarian community. This group consists of mostly capitalist farmers whose main objective of agricultural operation is to generate more marketable surplus from fixed arable land. They believe that it is possible through excessive application of chemical fertilizers to the land. With hope of more production surplus, they indiscriminately apply more chemical inputs to land along with increase of other variable factors. High subsidies on such inputs has become an inducing factor for them. These farmers are highly selfish and immoral in character so far as their business and production are concerned. Their commercial motives—more production—more marketable surplus—high profits—make them shortsighted and immoral in use and management of agrochemicals. While they use such inputs in lands, they rarely consider its adversities on the environment or on the interests of other farmers.

In sum, farmers' selfishness and commercial motive are the main causes of their moral degradation, which lead them towards a shortsighted resource management. Their tendency of overuse of chemical inputs in fixed arable land for maximisation of returns has caused environmental and ecological problems.

Technological Progress in Mining, Quarrying and Fishing Leading to Ecological Problems

Overexploitation of natural resources due to technological breakthrough in these fields and population pressure is found in many parts of the world. This has caused ecological and environmental problems in different manners. A vested group of people like contractors, tenants, companies, etc. with commercial motives exploit indiscriminately the natural common property resources such as forestry, minerals, fallow and fisheries. New technology transfer to these people has significantly contributed towards their operations.

In order to study the above matters, a sample survey was conducted by us in a few selected pockets of hill-tract and coastal areas of Balasore district in Orissa. Hill-tract villages, hills, forests, quarries, sea-beach villages, beach mangroves were visited by us, and villegers, contractors, *'thekedars'*, and other people who involved in the related activities in the above areas were interviewed through personal investigation. Findings are summarised as follows:

A. Unwarranted Expansion of Mining and Quarrying and Environmental Problems

In hill-tract areas, villagers, besides agriculture, largely depend on activities in forests, quarries and mines for their employment and income, especially during off-seasons of agriculture. Firewood collection, manual stone crushing, making statue and utensils from granites, etc. were the subsidiary activities of the people in earlier times. In traditional times, the people did not have any commercial motive for exploitation of forestry resources in these areas. Self-employment for subsistence earning for livelihood was the main objective of the all. Moreover, the traditional technology was not permitting people to have mass-exploitation of the forestry resources.

Towards late 1990s, a group of contractors had emerged from the hill-tract areas in the field of business of forestry and mining resources. The main motive of this group was to earn huge profits from the business. These contractors had easy access to the modern technology for exploitation of natural resources. The component of modern technology in the above field comprised compressors for drilling hills, highly explosive materials and remote-control devices for blasting giant stones and hills, modern stone crushing machines, bull-dozers, etc. In hill-tracts, many parts of hills and forests generally come under the jurisdiction of revenue department of the state government. For more revenue generation, the concerned revenue department leased out indiscriminately these hill areas to the above contractors on rental basis. Since the corrupt officials and local politicians extended their helping hands, the contractors found to have easy access to the overexploitation of forestry and mining resources by modern machinery.

Expansion of deforestation and quarrying operations and mushrooming of stone crushers amidst dense forests has occurred due to the intervention of the above contractors. This has not only threatened flora and fauna, but the tribal inhabitants dwelling in the surrounding areas have also been affected in different ways. Quarring and mining activities amidst dense forests and at high altitudes cause environmental problems in three ways. Firstly, for locating a quarry, on average, one-to-two hectares of forest areas is cleared which directly affect flora and bio-diversity. Secondly, due to crowd and interference of quarrymen at the forest sides, the inhabitations of wild animals and birds are severely disturbed and become quite unsafe. Thirdly, a large-scale deforestation and quarrying at high altitude cause massive soil erosion and landslide due to which small stones, sand and mud are flown down by rainwater and silted on cultivable lands. This damages crops and fertility of land. The cultivators in the surrounding areas in every year bear heavy cost of clearing these silts.

Besides the above problems, careless stone lastings by the contractors with new equipment very often cause stone-shot up of thousands of small pieces which scatter over around a half-mile radius, along with thunderous sound and vibration. The shotup stones reach villages and human settlement, and damage houses and kill/injure human, domestic and wild animals in these areas. Many *pacca* buildings in these areas are found cracked due to heavy vibration caused from stone blasting. The stonecrusher plants have become another headache for the people and farmers from the angle of pollution. Stonecrusher create environmental problems mainly in three ways: (i) emission of continuous flow of dust-particles-smoke from the plants pollutes the air in the surrounding area; (ii) blow of thunderous sound from the plants pollutes sound by which children are highly affected, and (iii) flow of stone-dust-particles from the crushers causes stone sedimentation on the nearby cultivable lands. According to farmers report, the arable lands surrounding a crusher plant are silted up to two-to-three inches thick annually by stone-dust blown from it. This significantly reduces the fertility of land.

B. Massive Deforestation and Clearance of Fallow Lands for Hill-side Cultivation

Recently, some groups of tribal people were found involved in clearing hill-slopes and fallow for cultivation. The access of new machinery to the hands of these people has induced them for cultivation in hill-tops and undulating hill-slopes and hill fallow. With the help of tractors and bull-dozers, the people deforest the vast areas of hill tops and slopes and forest fallow. A new variety of high yielding seeds is supplied to them which can be grown on highland. The forest is cleared and then it is fired for making space for cultivation. This process of cultivation is locally called *'puduchasa'*. Between Nilgiri and Devgiri hill ranges in Balasore district, there are about five hundred such 'puduchasa' farms located each one at the distance of half to one km. The average land area of each farm is about one acre. Again, in every 2-year interval, the farm location is shifted which is done again by clearing forest. According to our rough estimation, about 1500 acres of forest area have been cleared till now by the above community for 'puduchasa'. Cutting of timbers and burning of forest for 'puduchasa' have become daily events in these areas. This has tremendously increased ecological imbalance through air pollution, massive soil erosion, landslide and loss of bio-diversity.

In spite of repeated objections by the learned persons in the hill-tract areas, 'puduchasa' and deforestation are not yet stopped. Because this group of tribal farmers has commercial nexus with some unscrupulous contractors and local politicians those who indirectly support them. The local administrators are the silent spectators to this matter.

C. Sea-beach Deforestation, Deep-sea Fishing and Environmental Problems

In past, sea-beach forests were developed and preserved in order to protect the coastal arable lands from the effect of saline-sea-water which was very often thrown up by tides, and again, to lessen the velocity and intensity of marine cyclones. In recent years, like in other sea-coast areas, vast mangroves in sea-beach of Balasore had been severely damaged. Some contractors and farmers selecting sea-beach low-lands and shallow enclosed lands, where exchange of sweet and salty water is possible, have cleared coastal forest for the sake of shrimp cultivation. The growth of sea-food processing industries along coastal Orissa has inducted commercial motive in minds of the farmers and contractors. They have been highly encouraged for shrimp rearing by clearing vast mangroves in sea-beach areas. This has now caused a serious ecological problem in coastal areas of the state. Scientists believe that the devastation of human lives and properties in coastal Orissa during the last super cyclone in 1999 would be largely attributable to mass deforestation and ecological imbalance along the coast lines.

The technological breakthrough in the fields of deep-sea netting and fishing as well as in the areas of sea-food processing have helped fishermen to overexploit marine resources. As a result of deep-sea fishing and over crowd of sea-coast, many rare and endangered species of tortoise, fish and marine lives who inhabit in selected coasts for laying eggs and rearing, are now seriously affected. This has become a serious part of ecological problem and bio-diversity.

Overexploitation of common property resources in the above areas is happened on account of many factors. Among those, important factors are—selfishness and commercial motive of the exploiters leading them to lose ethical and moral values, competitive trend among them to grasp market gains, and their easy access to modern machinery and equipment. Overexploitation of resources neglecting human value consideration is the main cause of environmental pollution and ecological imbalance in the above areas.

Transgenic Crop Technology, Environment and Socio-Cultural Values

A new technological breakthrough has been recently made by biotechnologists in the area of seeds and plants breeding for agriculture. Biotechnologists have developed modern molecular biological methods by which extraction of genes from one variety plant and introducing the same into another variety was made possible. The plants/seeds developed by this method are known as transgenic plants (Sahai: 1994). The main objective of this technological invention is to raise plants' and seeds' self-resistance against diseases and pests, which would require less consumption of chemical pesticides. Consequently, the environmental hazards due to massive use of chemical pesticides in agriculture can be lessened.

Transgenic crops (TCs) have many advantages over the conventional HYVs. TCs are tolerant to herbicides, pests and insects. A gene from the soil bacterium bacillus thuringiensis (Bt) is inserted to transgenic seeds, which develops self-resistance to certain insects and pests. Therefore, TCs require least amount of chemical pesticides in crops and from that angle, the adversity of chemical pesticides is reduced. Besides, TCs are also resistant to draught, soil toxicity and salt (Qaim: 2001). These crops have proven high yield potential than the conventional HYVs.

Scientists have also warned that the TCs technology may prove to be more dangerous and hazardous than agrochemicals to the environment and mankind, if this is not carefully handled and regulated. One potential risk of the TCs is the possible loss of bio-diversity. The likelihood of transgenes escaping into the wild varieties through cross-pollination is generally higher in developing than developed countries (Qaim: 2001). Some superior transgenic crop varieties, in due course of time, can drive out the traditional varieties and local landraces, if the producers and consumers are completely biased towards TCs. A particular risk of Bt crops, expected by scientists, is that these crops may have detrimental effects on beneficial insects and on other non-target organisms. Bt crops produce a protein, which is highly toxic to pests (The Indian Express: 2001). There is possibility that as was happened with chemical pesticides, the pest population can develop resistance to the toxin produced by Bt genes. Consequently, it may not only entail Bt crop failure but the resistant pests may be more dangerous to non-Bt crops. Another adversity on the ecosystem expected in TCs is that it may narrow down the genetic base of agro-bio-diversity region. The narrowing of the genetic base increases vulnerability of crops of single-gene-based pathogenes so that genetic uniformity increases danger of famine (Nachane: 1995). Again, since Bt produces a highly toxic protein for killing pests, it may be hazardous to human, animals and birds consuming it.

Unfortunately, the TCs technology has been developed and controlled by the private multinational companies mostly originating from developed countries. In earlier times, particularly in the USA, plant improvement research was to a large extent carried out in public organisations. With advent of modern biotechnology, the private sector significantly gained importance. Because the capital requirement for investment in such technological research was so huge and high risky that the public sector institutions even in developed nations were reluctant to invest in such lines. At the global level, between 75 to 80 per cent of all R and D investment in agricultural biotechnology was made by private multinational companies (Qaim: 2001). Since the objectives of private MNCs are completely commercial *i.e.* to raise profits from technology and have economic control over the world, there is greater chance of misuse of this technology. With these objectives, the MNCs very often deviate from human values and environmental considerations while they involve in the business of technology transfer to developing countries.

Recently, the patent laws of the World Trade Organisation (WTO) particularly for the transgenic plants strengthened the bussiness-holds of the MNCs at global level. The agreement on Trade Related Intellectual Property Rights (TRIPs) was an integral part of the WTO agreement concluded among 117 countries including India, in 1994 at Marrakesh. In this agreement, patenting of life-forms such as of plants and naturally occurring genes, as was proposed by Arthur Dunkel, was added to the patent regime. All member countries were to harmonize their domestic patent laws with the WTO-TRIPs regime. Granting monopoly rights through 'patent' to the MNCs on the transgenic crop technology and on other living organisms not only provides legal rights to overexploit the germplasm resources of the developing countries, but the entire farmers community in these countries is also exploited by the MNCs in different ways.

The objectives and business operations of MNCs in the transgenic technology are not harmonized with human values and socio-cultural and economic values of the farmers. Owing to that, their technology transfers to less developed and poor countries had implications of technological adversities on the environment and socio-cultural-economic values in those countries. In developing countries, the farmers are morally deprived of their rights on own resources, such as on preservation of seeds from own crops, selling of seeds to their brothers, etc. In many instances, the MNCs have displayed their anti-moral and anti-human activities in transgenic technology business. Piracy of germplasm from the tropical regions (which are very rich in bio-diversity and gerplasm resources) by the MNCs agents are reported frequently. There are ample instances of usage of 'terminator' genes in transgenic seeds by the MNCs. 'Monsanto', the U.S. based seeds corporation, has introduced 'terminator' genes into its transgenic seeds (Thomas, *et al.*: 1994). The terminator genes prohibit plants generating productive potential seeds. That means the seeds preserved from one crop cannot be used for the next crop. So that the farmers would have to buy seeds for every harvest. They will be perennially dependent on MNCs for their seeds requirement. Such manipulation in technology completely goes against the human values, particularly socio-economic ethics of the farmers. The groups of petty, marginal and small farmers are the most sufferers under such technological transfer. Many environmentalists, mainly from less developed countries, have very strongly objected to the WTO patent regime on life forms such as on transgenic crops. The entire process of patenting on life forms, as they viewed, is aimed at shifting the process of knowledge-generation and technological knowhow from farming communities to private companies mainly to MNCs. Under the WTO-IPR regime, there is an unequal and free-flow of bio-diveristy from developing countries' informal sectors to the developed countries' organized private corporate sectors (Vandana: 1992 and Thomas, *et al.*: 1994).

By and large, commercial and monopolistic motives of the private multinational companies in the fields of research, development and business of technology transfer have made them shortsighted and unscrupulous. They frequently deviate from human value considerations while they involve in such business. Consequently, detachment of human value judgement from transgenic crop technology frequently leads the technology to reveal its harmful effects on the environment and human health.

Conclusion and Suggestion

Technological breakthrough in primary sector was necessitated in order to enhance the productive potential of the sector for coping with increased demand for food stuff and infrastructure due to over-pressure of population. But, of late, change in human psychology towards selfishness and shortsightedness in resource management and usage of technology became the main cause of overexploitation and environmental problems. Under such change, moral values in human started to diminish. Farmers and contractors operating in the primary sector started to misuse and mishandle the risky technologies for the fulfilment of their commercial objectives.

In agriculture, mostly the capitalist farmers in the developed regions overexploited the fixed land resource applying excessive chemical inputs to it. Consequently, this caused environmental and ecological problems. In mining, quarrying and fishing, new technology transfer to the group of unscrupulous contractors became the important cause of massive deforestation, soil erosion and consequently, ecological imbalance both in hill-tract and coastal areas. As regards new technological breakthrough in the fields of seeds and plants, the private multinational companies had monopolistic control over the entire process, starting from invention to application through WTO-patent regime. Since the main objectives of MNCs rarely complied with socio-economic ethics and human value norms in less-developed countries, MNCs business dealings, especially in the area of transgenic crop technology, led to many socio-economic and environmental problems.

In sum, objectives of technological development and transfer were on the verge of being completely detached from the human value and environmental considerations. Consequently, the new technology, specifically in primary sector has become an important factor for the environmental degradation and human health hazard, besides socio-cultural and economic adversities.

Foreseeing the future situations in population growth, demand for foodstuff, employment and socio-cultural changes, the world must need technological breakthrough in various fields of economic activities. One obsolete technology is to be replaced by a new one. Technology transfer across regions/ countries is necessary for a balanced development at the global level. The maladies of technology and science can be minimized if scientists and nations undertake certain precautions towards it.

Technological and scientific research, development and transfer in any field should be bestowed upon human value systems. These must be harmonized with human noble desires and needs. Hence, a spiritual and holistic approach to scientific inventions would be correct step towards the above. Excessive profit motive behind a technological invention is very dangerous to the environment and human as it leads to overexploitation of both natural and human resources. The research organisations as well as the concerned governments should be very watchful so that any risky technology must not be transferred to any unscrupulous persons or institutions. Besides, creation of awareness and training among people about environment and ecology would be necessary steps. The educational system and curriculum are to be designed in such a line that the students' enlightenment and seriousness towards human value systems will be possible.

References

Dahiya, L.N. (1996), "Agrochemicals, Food and Environmental Issues in India: An Overview" in proceedings of IAAE Symposium on "Economics of Agrochemicals" held at Wageningen, The Netherlands, April 24-27, 1996.

Gaur, G. (1997), *Water Polllution and Its Management*, Sarup and Sons, New Delhi.

Gracy, C.P., *et al.* (1996), "Towards Sustainable Farming Practices – A Changing Trend in Agro-chemicals Use in Southern Karnataka" in proceedings of IAAE, *op cit*.

Jerry, L. Holechek, *et al.* (2000), *Natural Resources: Ecology, Economics and Policy*, Prentice-Hall, USA.

Jindal, R. and Singh, J. (1989), "Toxicity of Pesticides to the Productivity of a Fresh Water Pond", *Indian Journal of Environmental Health*, Vol. 31, No. 3.

Karpagam, M. (1991), *Environmental Économics: A Text Book*, Sterling, New Delhi.

Majumdar, D.K. (1994), "Nutrients and Water Management for Sustainable Agriculture and Environment", *Agricultural Situation in India*.

Miller, G.T. (1990), *Resource Conservation and Management*, Belmont, C.A. Wadsworth Publishing Co.

Mohapatra, K.M. (2001), "Green Revolution Technology and Some Environmental Issues: A Note on Indian Experience" paper presented in Prof. D.R. Gadgil Birth Centenary Year National Seminar, April 8-9, GIPE, Pune, is under publication.

Mohapartra, K.M. and Kavita Srivastava (2002), "WTO Agreements, Prospect of Agriculture and Environment: In the Context of India", presented in Orissa Economic Association – Annual Conference, is under publication in *Orissa Economic Journal*.

Mohapatra, K.M. and Nisha Sharma (2001), "Switching Over to Non-phosphatic Detergents and Feasible Economic Policy Options: The Case of Kanpur", in edited book *Detergents and the Environment: The Canadian Experience* and the *Indian Scenario* by Clive Southy *et al.* Tata McGraw-Hill Publishing Company Limited, New Delhi.

Nachane, D.M. (1995), "Intellectual Property Rights in Uruguay Round: An Indian Prospective", *Economic and Political Weekly*, XXX, No. 5, Feb. 4.

Qaim, Matin (2001), "Transgenic Crops and Developing Countries", *Economic and Political Weekly*, Vol. XXXVI, No. 32, Aug. 11.

Sahai, Suman (1994), "Intellectual Property Rights for Life Form", *Economic and Political Weekly*, Vol. XXIX, No. 3, Jan. 15.

Sengupta, R. (2001), *Ecology and Economics: An Approach to Sustainable Development*, Oxford University Press, New Delhi.

The Indian Express (2001), Oct. 21, Oct. 28 and Nov. 2.

Thomas, P. *et al.* (1994), "Dunkel Text: Implications for Rural Secor", *Economic and Political Weekly*, Vol. XXIX, No. 13, March 26.

Vandana, Shiva and Crompton, Tom (1998), "Monopoly and Monoculture – Trends in Indian Seed Industry: *Economic and Political Weekly*, Sept. 26.

Venkateshwarlu, J. (1985), "Ecological Crisis in Agro-ecosystems" in edited book *Indian's Environmental:* Crisis *and Responses* by Bandyopadyay, J., *et al.*, Natraj Publishers, Dehradun.

SECTION IV

IMPACT OF INFORMATION AND COMPUTER TECHNOLOGY ON HUMAN VALUES

18

Towards Information Society

V.K. Jain

Introduction

Information technology (IT) has transformed us to the 'information age' and is building information society. The main indicators of information society are right time, information rather than the capital as a strategic resource base, shift of occupational structure from manufacturing to information base activities, and a well developed infrastructure. The challenges posed before information society in our country are lack of adequate infrastructure, especially in smaller towns and rural areas, information management skills, up-to-date subject knowledge and proper information policy. IT is the fastest growing science today. Internet is exploding at a rate of 10-12 per cent per month. IT provides tremendous benefits like fast exchange of information, filling of information and knowledge gaps, online shopping and e-transaction etc. But, like any other technology, it is not free from misuse. Some people abuse Internet for e-crimes, vulgarity and violence etc.

There is a need to make the benefits of IT and Internet available to masses, especially the poor in rural sector and, at the same time, preventing its abuse by imbibing moral and spiritual values in the youth.

Information technology (IT), which has evolved from convergence of computers and telecommunication, has led to a revolution just like industrial revolution of Second World War and the computer revolution of 1960s. Both revolutions have resulted in freeing the man from physical and clerical labour and in increasing his leisure time. IT is the fastest growing science known today. Over the last four decades, digital revolution has taken us to the era of IT revolution. It has brought about a sea-change in the way people exchange information. It has transformed us to the 'information age' and has built an information society. The new information society (IS) combines both continuity and fundamental change. The core tenet of the IS is the utilisation and exploitation of information for overall development of human beings. The significant indicators of the information society are:

- Right access to right information at the right time.
- Information rather than the capital as a strategic resource base.
- Shift in occupational structure from manufacturing to information base activities.
- A well developed IT infrastructure.

Challenges faced in making IS in 21st century are lack of good IT infrastructure, information management skills, up-to-date subject knowledge, proper information policy and intellectual property rights.

Internet, which is a loose connection of several thousand computer networks, has grown enormously and is still growing at an amazing rate of 10-12 per cent per month. Its significance is felt globally far greater than its predecessors such as the printing press, telephone and even the television. What radio took 25 years and TV 14 years to reach as many people as Internet, the Internet has done it in just 5 years. The present Internet user base exceeds 150 million. In the US alone, it has recently crossed the 100 million mark. In India, it is around 2.3 million in 1999. It was forecasted that by the end of the year 2003, the number would increase to 70 million. By then, Internet penetration will be just 6 per cent compared to 33 per cent in Singapore and 58 per cent in Taiwan. It is thus abundantly clear that there is a vast untapped potential for the growth of IT in India. It is an opportunity, which our country cannot and should not afford to miss. Like any other technology, IT has both bright and dirty faces. Bright in the sense that it has made communication easier, cheaper and in the reach of the largest number of persons, filled communication and knowledge gaps, made the world borderless, removed trade barriers and improved quality of life; and dirty in the sense that it has led to high tech cheating, birth of e-crimes, vulgarity and violence and abundance of pornographic material on the screen. The benefits of IT far outweigh its misuse. IT is a tool, it is up to the man to use it for good or bad. We must make its use for the benefit of the largest section of the society, especially the poor ones rather than indulge in e-crimes and sexual vulgarity, which will lead us to nowhere.

Information Technology for Improving Quality of Life

The development of knowledge through experience has contributed enormously to quality of life. IT has played a great role in spreading knowledge. Today, voluminous literature on any subject is available on the Internet. It is quickest source of making literature search on any topic from history, religion, medicine to computer and IT itself. The various applications of IT for bettering human life are discussed below:

(a) Agriculture

It might be surprising to know that the Internet is being used even in agriculture. The farmers in developed countries make use of information from remote sensing, geographical information systems (GIS) and global positioning systems (GBS) to detect early pests and diseases, and accordingly, apply the right quantities of pesticides, fertilizers and water at the right time. Besides, computers are being used for farm and scare water management. Information about weather forecast is also quickly available on Internet. Today, we hear about genetic revolution, which has resulted in abundance of pest free crops. Without application of modern IT, the large population, especially in India, cannot be properly fed.

(b) Service Sector

Service sector has perhaps benefited most from IT. Applications in this sector range from e-mail, entertainment (Web TV), electronic publishing and distribution, online shopping, online reservation, job search, matrimonial services, health services, travel services, news, etc. to e-commerce.

Banking sector has recently undergone computerzation in a big way. Branches in the cities and metros are connected through network and physical banking is losing much of its meaning with the onset of virtual banking. Virtual banking will provide instant access to customers from anywhere on the globe.

These days hospital information systems are also being developed. Hospitals keep patients' records on computers. Expert medical diagnosis/advice is available on Internet. One can quickly seek international experts' opinion on the Internet by feeding textual and graphic test reports of the patients. Yet, comparatively, a little has been contributed towards development of IT infrastructure for health system Medicos. Medicos demand a greater IT usage in heath systems and suggest a five stage IT infrastructure for development of health systems.

(c) Business

The Internet economy is growing at the rate of 100 per cent per year. The growth rate of e-commerce is awesome. This year (1999), goods worth $30 billion are expected to be sold by Internet and it was expected to cross $250 billion mark by end of the year 2002. Indian Market Research Bureau estimated that by the year 2001 e-commerce in India would range between Rs. 29,000 and Rs. 67,000 crores.

Internet is also impacting our daily life. Internet users can bargain airfares and look for maximum discounts on almost all products. There are shopping malls and bargain bazars on satyamonline.com, rediff.com and timesofindia.com etc. The beneficiaries of Internet are both suppliers and consumers. It provides a level playing field to all businessmen irrespective of their sizes. The customer's advantage is cost effectiveness. A small businessman can set up his stall on the internet and sell goods to customers all over the world just like any large MNC. India's most valuable companies are already dawn of .com era. Many entreprenuers have succeeded in launching business web-sites on Internet in the country and there is a business on the Internet for everybody. Business on Internet has shrunk gestation period from 1/100 to 1/10 of the physical world. To cite an example, yahoo.com took just 5 years to reach the same market capitalisation as General Motors of USA did in 100 years. It is thus an ideal rather inevitable tool for business.

(d) Education

One of the biggest beneficiaries of the Internet is education. The World Wide Web (WWW) has brought significant change in teaching-learning strategies in the last 5 years. In advanced countries, every student has either his own PC with Internet connectivity or has easy access to the Internet. Teachers leave their notes and give assignments on the Home Page. Students can study them at their own pace and make self evaluation. Besides, they can find relevant articles and books on a particular topic in cyber space. Video conferencing can stimulate discussions among students, teachers and peers. In near future, National Education Network connecting computer LANs of educational institutions will be formed. IT based learning thus offers the advantage of self-pace learning with self-evaluation, video conferencing, use of virtual reality for experiments and exploration and sharing of expensive resources between the institutions. Distance education is also spreading its wings in India. IGNOU has taken a lead in this direction. It is offering a number of courses on Internet through more than 700 centres. For lively classroom teaching, interactive channels and satellite links can be used.

A successful experiment of fast learning of children in India from Internet has been performed by Mitra and Rana. It was observed that even the unprivileged students learn computer operation very fast. They suggested to install a large base of

PC kiosks with internet connectivity in urban areas and PCs with wireless connectivity in other areas.

A host of career guidance services are also available on the Internet. Websites like reddif.com, margdarshan.com etc. offer efficient career guidance service in the country. Several spiritual sites are also available on the Internet.

Indian Scene

India is not lagging behind in Internet usage. VSNL introduced commercial Internet access in India in 1995. The present user base has grown to 2.3 million. Presently, the Internet is confined to affluent population in the metropolis. The Government of India has identified IT as one of the thrust areas and taken several steps to promote IT industry. Tamil Nadu Government has decided to make entire state computer literate in a span of 10 years. It means that computer education will be provided in all schools, colleges, universities and other educational institutions.

As we all know, the state of Andhra Pradesh is being transformed into IT state. Personal records of all individuals, land and government records are being kept on computer. Karnataka state has created an independent department of IT and has set up a task force to boost IT sector in the state. The department is trying to establish a communication backbone reaching down to the taluk. It is offering fiscal incentives for IT business in the state. It has even set up a bilingual Net portal and e-commerce site to enable rural traders to transact over the Internet. To allow easy public accesses to government information on the website, IT kiosks are being set up statewide. Recently, the state of Kerala has taken initiative to computerize all government departments, thus entering in the fields of e-governance. It has chalked out intensive plan to train government officials and teachers in higher secondary schools. Other states are also chalking out massive computerization plans.

With the new telecommunication policy, many ISPs (Internet Service Providers) are laying backbones and citywide networks in major metros and cities. By the end of this year (1999), some 70 cities are likely to be covered by Internet. Our country has immense potential to use Internet. It can multiply foreign trade and improve quality of life of masses. Social scientists say that security of a nation has direct bearing on better living. It is said that the country that is most secure is the one whose citizens are having better living standards. India must wake up to new millennium by joining廣Internent bandwagon in a big way. We must transform ourselves to information society.

Misuse of Internet

IT is rapidly polluting our civilisation, rich traditions, high moral and spiritual values. It has given birth to high tech e-crimes, virtual nudity, violence, vulgarity and has made people, especially the children, Internet addict. E-mail users receive a huge junk mail. Innocent children and students easily get attracted to sexual websites.

Balanced Approach Needed

There is no doubt that IT and Internet in particular has contributed significantly to the physical development of man. Modern IT has turned the world into a village, communication services have developed beyond imagination, business is growing at the speed of thought, and quality of life has improved. But the use of IT is confined to a selected few, especially in our country where computers and Internet are available to the affluent few in metropolis. Currently, the penetration of PC in India is merely 3.2 million. We must devise means by which the benefits of IT can be brought to the masses, especially to the poor. There is a need to adopt a balanced approach in education to imbibe moral and spiritual values in the youth. We must wake up to the call of information society, build up a good infrastructure, establish a vast base of PC kiosks with wireless connectivity in rural areas and make these services available to the poor at affordable rates. Then only we shall be building a true information society for overall development of the human beings.

References

Gill, N.S. and Dabas, K.C. (1999), "Challenges Before Information Society", *University News*, Vol. 37 (12), March 22, pp. 17-23.

Bedi, S. and Saini, H.S. (1999), "Stages of IT Usage in a State Health System Corporation", *CSI Communications*, Vol. 23 (4), October, pp. 9-37.

Business Today, September 7 1999, "India's Most Valuable Companies".

Business World, September 6 1999, There is a Business on the Net for You (1999), .

Mitra, S. and Rana, V. (1999), "Children and the Internet: An Experiment with Minimally Invasive Education in India", *CSI Communications*, Vol. 22 (12), June, pp. 12-16.

19

Preserving Human Values in Information Technology Era

B. Vijaya Mary, K. Krishna Priya and *M. Subbarayudu*

Man is ever conscious about his self-improvement. The ideal of a "better state of living" is only known to human being is not known to any other species of the creation. We see in our day-to-day development that man's energy is employed in a variety of ways. Man is capable of integrating the past with the present and the present with the future.

This integrating power is a part of his natural legacy, and it is not acquired through the process of technological development. Man's creative power is more developed. Scientific and technological education has widened a man's vision. They are considered to be powerful integrating mediums in modern times. The world today is not the same as it was years ago. For building a dynamic and progressive society, science and technology play important roles. The development of knowledge through experience contribute enormously to the quality of life.

Scientific brains claim to conquer the forces of the nature *e.g.* land, water and air. By our scientific brains, we enjoy greater command over natural resources *vis-a-vis* technological development.

As an illustration, in a country like India where farming is an important occupation, technology plays an important role. Emerging farming techniques are based on precision farming methods leading to plant scale rather than field scale industry. Farmers in industrialised countries, using information from remote sensing, geographical information system (GIS), global positioning system (GPS), and information and computer technologies, are able to detect early pests and diseases and are targeting the application of pesticides, fertilizers and water to those parts of the fields that need them urgently.

Similarly, biotechnology, another important aspect, helps in strengthening food, water and health security systems. And other three major revolutions in science and technology which influence agriculture and industry in a fundamental manner are:

(i) Gene revolution,
(ii) Eco technology, and
(iii) Information and communication revolution.

Speaking about the above third revolution, it is widely used in processing large capacity of database for increasing research productivity for understanding agro ecosystems and remote sensing for geographical information which have become elements of the "science and technology for the basic human needs" movement.

But are these fruits of technological developments reaching every man? The large segment of world's population is awaiting for the fruits of science on one hand, and a massive market interest is growing to grave the science for profit motive, on the other. That is, at one level, the traditional barriers are diminishing and, on the other, the market forces are creating new institutional barriers to separate science from the public. So, unlike any other society, Indian society has reached a complex socio-economic and cultural stage. The literacy is very low. Only a thin section of society is aware of frontiers in science, which includes information technology and bio-technology. Even politically, world is losing its stability. Diplomatic relations are so worst that single a match stick can lead to destruction. The world as a whole is becoming speed conscious and materialistic. The societies as a whole and individually are reacting according to their socio-cultural positions and assumptions rather than critical evaluation. Here the question of human values arises.

What are human values actually? They have multiple dimensions and have diverse roles to play. Truth, love, tolerance, selfless service, social good, etc. are real ethical ideals without which man can never be a complete individual. For the development of these qualities, a proper system of education is necessary. The aim of education should be to enable the youth to make his or her living, to equip them to play their part as citizens of democracy. Education is training for citizenship as much as training the mind. It is, in short, meant to enjoy a good life. This is lacking today, so the consequence of improper education is finding its ways in the wrong usage of technological fruits.

The technically qualified man is deserting his discipline only because of money. Scientists and technically trained people are lost in their craving for money that they are either brain-drained or deserting their disciplines for management and software. Due to the rapid technological development, man is becoming so money-minded that an alarming number of our technologists are deserting the chosen professions, which is not only depleting the pool of technologists but also degrading purpose for which the technical institutes are made. A consciousness of "better life"is driving most of the eligible engineers and technologists to brain-drain. As the pool of good engineers gets increasingly depleted, imitation and import will be viewed as comfortable but eventually dangerous solution.

India, in the recent years, has developed and, is still in the process of development. A number of examples for it can be quoted. One of these is Pokhran tests which have been conducted successfully. The world today has become so tense that every country, big or small, vast or narrow, needs power defensive tool which is none other than nuclear bombs. Similarly, like any other nation, India has right and freedom to pursue nuclear deterrence in self-defence. No one can question that. But the real issue is that does the security of nation exist only in the conventional force and nuclear power? Does not an average Indian who lives in poverty requires sufficient food, shelter and security for his life? The country that is most secure is the one whose citizens have better living. For diverting or decreasing the amount being spent on nuclear bombs does not only depend on single constituency or single nation, but also it is the responsibility of the whole world to follow a single path of love, peace and respect for its neighbours. Every country should respect the security of its neighbours. And this is possible only when the people and the politician have in themselves the character of a good human.

In India 60 per cent of the population is barefoot and in every summer, people die of heat stroke for lack of water. If only the people of upper cadre and posts could think about these human problems with love and kindness as a whole, then only time and huge amounts of money being wasted on nuclear weapons all over the world could be used for the common good of every man.

Considering a society and the influences of various media, in particular, TV, a powerful medium of information, should be programmed properly as to:

- Provide good entertainment;
- Transfer good schemes on education;
- Highlight the importance of good character, sincerity, leadership qualities, accommodative nature, transparent behaviour, right approach for community development and good living; and
- Have programmes which bring the importance of unity in diversion, group activity for the overall development of human living condition, but the programmes in TV are taking the youth in different directions. Even parents and elders are not giving due consideration for the well being of their kith and kin.

The pervasive poverty we witness today is the most serious indictment of contemporary development pathways. The poor, as they have no productive assets like land, education, any technical skills, etc., earn their livelihood largely through unskilled work. They have been bypassed by modern technical advances, and suffer from sense of exclusion from the exciting scientific adventures that we are witnessing today. So reaching the unreached and including the excluded have to be important concepts of science and technological policy and strategy for the new millennium. If the huge stock of scientific and technological knowledge and innovations with which we will be entering the new millennium is to become a blessing for the human kind as a whole, then the following points should be considered.

The first step is to narrow down the vast "knowledge gap". The scientists must spread their skills and values throughout their own nations through local communications. Taking full advantage of new information technology, one should use it for the well being of the common man.

The brain-drain of engineers and scientists can be minimized by awarding and encouraging young scientists. An opportunity should be given to them in order to awaken their inner talents.

Women are considered to be the weaker section of the society in India. It can be seen that even science curricula are biased. If only a chance is given to them to participate actively, it would lead to a balanced society. If a woman gets opportunity to be educated, the entire family and children are moulded into good citizens.

Technological development and materialistic views of human beings are racing almost at equal pace. However, human values such as tolerance, love, accommodative nature, brotherhood, service attitude etc. are decreasing exponentially. If this process continues, a situation may come that the life on this noble earth may be unbearable. So, there must be a balance between the technological development and human values. For that, everybody must work collectively so that the living conditions will be good. There must be change in minds of every human being on the earth, which we have always dreamt of.

20

Information and Computer Technology and its Relation to Human Values

Sanjeev Batra

Introduction

Human values concern chiefly with the advancement of men's welfare in such a manner that basic human attributes can be conserved. It is because for survival, what you need more than anything else are ethics and morals. Everyone in this world wants to be contended with one's lot. So the ultimate aim of human is to achieve happiness, which is the natural state of human being. But again this aim has two groups of attributes, namely, internal attributes which interest one basically known as *'Swadharma'* and the other group of external attributes which are slightly higher than the basic needs. All actions which are performed to fulfill the goals set by above attributes are known as duties. Duties are nothing but moral or legal obligations, what one is bound or ought to do.

Question about information and computer technology today in the coming centenary arises due to their adverse impacts on the human being. Technological progress does not necessarily bring about social advancement. It may well have negative consequence. It threatens human existence through affecting his values and civilisation.

'*Mantra*' of Information Technology

Today's world is of information and computer technology. The information and computer technology has shaken the whole world. We are in the age of re-invention in quick succession. Man has invented many electronic devices but the computer has made a greater impact on the society than others. The computer has made a potentially significant contribution to the society during the last three decades. Thanks to the internet, it seems easier to forge human relationships and easier to hide the real world. This virtual world makes it possible to avoid good old fashioned honesty in relationships. There is an adage that is 'when in doubt, be honest'. But there may be some codicils, 'don't be honest if you think it is going to hurt someone'.

Whatever was good earlier seems to be harmful in this compuage. What is more important is the urgency in updating the laws to cover the internet environment. It is the environment which definitely makes you sit on your chair and then let you move around the world. With the help of computers, now, one can purchase anything by ordering it on the internet from his home. This has positive as well as negative aspects. If talk about the benefits, then this will ensure the saving of time and efforts, while, on the other hand, it will make a man idle.

The Optimistic Outlook

One hundred years from now, historians will consider the present development of computer technology as a major human achievement. But they may also conclude in future decades that computer was a machine that people had not yet learned how to use it. These historians may instead admit one thing that people had developed some effective data processing, and had only begun to realise the computer's potential in more important areas *i.e.* in the areas which improve the quality of life and the well-being of the people. Optimistic forecasters believe that greater freedom and individuality and a more human and personalized society will result from future computer applications.

Greater Freedom and Individuality

The optimistic view of the future is that greater freedom and individuality are encouraged by the use of computers. Optimists foresee no insurmountable problems in the society adapting to the changes brought about by increased computer utilisation. The greater productivity that resulted in computer usage will lead to an increased standard of living, a shorter work week, and increased leisure time. Although it will be a challenge for human beings to put aside age-old attitudes towards work and learn to use creatively the free time they will have in the future, the optimists believe that people can learn to use their leisure in ways that are contemplative and self-fulfilling.

Also it is argued, people will be freed from the basic struggle to maintain their existence and will have the time and resources to pursue the activities of their choice. Since individuality has been defined as the freedom to exercise choice according to one's own scale of performace, it will thus be enhanced.

More Human and Personalized Society

Optimists also believe that the sophisticated computer systems of the future will permit a more human and personalized society, that will further reduce the need for individual conformity. They argue that the complexity at our present society, the millions of people crowded into it, and the inadequacy of our present information systems act to encourage conformity and thus to restrict personalization and human freedom of choice. However, when sophisticated information sysyems are developed and widely used to handle routine transactions, it will be possible to focus greater personal attention on exceptional transactions.

Deterioration in Human Values

Although computer systems can help people in countless ways, yet it is also possible to have a negative impact on some individuals. Some of the potential adverse effects such as the dehumanzing of the society and the loss of individual privacy often attributed to computer systems may often be the subtle consequences of complex and interrelated technological forces operating in a society with a growing population density. Also, computers, being inanimate objects, do not wrong, but the people who use them sometimes do.

(a) Technology's Devil in Mass Media

The re-invention concept of information technology and computers have had a full grip over the whole world. But the only thing lacks in it is the revival of human values. In the sphere of mass communication, information technology can also promote destructive processes. It can be, and has been, used to distort messages as well as to disseminate them more widely and accurately than before.

Distorting news and information is not new. It has been attempted over the centuries by countries and groups hostile to each other, and by ruling groups to deceive their own people. But the objectives of old-fashioned propaganda were largely limited to securing advantages for one group over another. What disturbs today is the increasing ability of sophisticated modern technology to make it possible to package information for ulterior purposes, to use it as a vehicle for marketing products.

To blame technology for deterioration in the media may be unfair, for it is a tool. But it whets the temptation to use the latest devices in colour printing; in type and design, in transforming, even fictionalizing, photographs; in preferring pre-packaged news and entertainment features, to make up for poor content.

(b) Effect of Internet

Internet has brought the whole world closer. The pessimist's view of internet is that the effects of it has been to damage human values, and they foresee increasingly harmful trends. Internet will tend to dominate our lives. We may be swept away along with a technological tide and we shall have little control over the harassed victims of a depersonalized and dehumanized process.

Internet has made a man less social and less outgoing which adversely affect the preservation of human values. Also, the contemporary views are that computers and technology are an unbridled curse-holds as technology increases unemployment, leads to depersonalization and bewilderment, threatens an individuals's right to dignity and privacy, and threatens to pollute and/or blow up the world. This view is deficient, although it probably contains an element of truth.

Conclusion

The human life today deviates from the worthiness lying inside it. Due to innovation of technology, the whole scenario seems to be changed. The human life is shifting from spiritualism to materialism. The tendency of human life is leading towards excessive materialism under which influence the human is now becoming highly selfish, shortsighted and self-centred. The impact of technology has weiled the real worth lies hidden deep inside everyone at the core of human being. External covering may be shiny and attractive but as far as one is concerned this is not very important; it is what is inside you that really matters. Yes many people, specially in our consumerist world of today, concentrate on the exterior alone.

21

Impact of IT on Human Values

A Balanced View

Manu Pratap Singh, C.M. Mishra and *V.K. Saraswat*

Introduction

The famous stories of Mahabharata about Arjun hitting the eye of a fish with extreme accuracy by seeing its shadow in a tub of oil while the fish was fastly rotating above a rotating wheel or about Sanjay telling the living telecast of the huge battle field to the Dhratrastra describing every minute event in details, looked like scientific fictions of recent inventions of super fast computers and ultrahigh communication system like 'Information Technology'. With the outgrowth of electronics in the form of computer technology and the communication through information technology, there is no reason to disbelieve the possibility of such historical events. Fifty year ago, British mathematician Alan M. Turing predicted that by the turn of the century, computers would be able to think. As the new millennium approaches, computer scientists have yet to create a computer that can pass this Turing's test. But they are getting nearer to that. Some like research scientist Jim Gray and his colleagues in the data base research field have made great strides in transforming the computer into a better repository of human knowledge. A senior research and manager of Microsoft's Bay Area Research Centre (MBARC), Gray's work over the past three decades has made it possible for computers to store and analyse ever larger amounts of information. As a result of his research, database have evolved from 10 megabytes-sized storage facilities, which were the sole property of large corporations and government institutions, into terabyte-sized computers available in millions of people. His work paved the way for many of daily transactions we now take for granted, such as withdrawing money from automatic teller machines (ATMs), railway/airlines reservations and purchasing products on internet. Three months ago, the Association of Computer Machines (ACM) awarded Gray, the prestigious A.M. Turing award, for his contributions to information technology. This award is widely regarded in industry circle as the Nobel Prize of Computer Science. Gray received this award for his contributions to database and transaction processing research and technical relationship in system implementation from research prototypes to commercial products.

Recently developed Net-Telephony (almost free telephone call system) harness the strength of two key technologies *i.e.,* the NET and telecommunication network, in bringing to our desktop the power or real time communication. It requires a PC with sound capability, a NET connection, speakers, microphones and telephony software such as Media Ring. In the process of high tech cricket, Bobwoolmer (the tech-savvy cricket coach of South African cricket team) is well-known for leading on cricket field with all kinds of calculation through his laptop. Recently developed digit lock speaks Sudh Hindi and classical 'Sanskrit' too. This software (available in www.dwelle.de) tells time in 35 languages that the service broadcasts. There have been several other exciting innovative technologies for comfort, benefit and service of human race in the field of education, research, medical science, industry, commerce and communications. To quote a few, we now have high-tech stethoscope where electronics has been added to world's oldest most trusted and popular diagnostic medical instrument. We have now a very reliable system (mirror in pipe line) for managing and restoring data traffic flowing across high capacity optical network, and we also have the process of virtual reality where ride at Disneyland moves us through real three dimensional space, but the ride is always the same and always predictable. Such virtual reality gives us control of where we go, what we do and to whom we encounter (we have 3-D freedom). A recent trend of computer generated movies have also been started, through which the computers as camara has clicked with resounding success in the film industry. In the Hollywood picture 'flick, the bug's life', a Disney Picture Production, the main character is a human like bug called Flick whose head is the digitized version of clay scripture and body shaped with three dimensional animation system special effects through computer generated animation. Imaging has become the recent trend in Indian film industry also. With new multimedia, the time and cost in film production and broadcasting is plunging, providing better scope for special effects. These days, even the advertisements come along with animation and computer graphics images on our television sets.

Besides all these revolution brought by computer and information technologies in all fields of civilised life, the fact remains that every manufactured product and its concerned technology in its uses have both positive and negative effects on life and environment, and the lack of proper value judgement makes the negative effects more pronounced. It creates imbalances between materialism and idealism and leaves adverse effects on human value system.

Positive Effects of Computer and Information Technologies

(a) Internet Connectivity

Using satellite communication system through Internet, the different parts of the country can be connected for the purpose of very effective administration, financial control, crime control, family planning and healthcare, education, research, communications, agricultural revolution, weather forecasting, etc. In education system the following arrangements can be made:

(i) Establishing connectivity among all universities.
(ii) Establishing connectivity of all teaching departments

of university or a research institute with its central library.

(iii) Establishing connectivity of central library of a university with International Information Centre through world web to exchange the research developments and teaching methodology in various subsets and different branches of education in international level.

Using this connectivity, the researchers of various fields will have activities at par with any international centre of higher learning and research without making investments in such as international research journal's ever-increasing cost. Using this connectivity, the update information can be sought about advanced sophisticated rare instruments and techniques and use of rare high level books, periodicals and journals can be made. This connectivity can also be used to search the possibilities of international competitions and job opportunities for the students in every branch of knowledge.

(b) Distance Education by Internet

Indian Space Research Organization (ISRO) in 1975 conducted satellite instruction television experiment (SITE) for mass education in various fields like agricultural programme, family welfare and health services in 2400 villages. As such, education and training through satellite are not new things in India. The experimental non-formal distance education using this technique is becoming a reality in our country. As such, India has come up with the second largest open university in the whole world. In this direction Indira Gandhi National Open University (IGNOU) is using this distance education system in more than 700 telecommunication centres through inset satellite with a brilliant track record of bringing higher education to the remote areas of the country. IGNOU is now fast catching up the web train. It has moved one step closer towards launching a virtual university campus.

It is believed that education is complete only when student

has the opportunity to interact with the teacher. To meet this end, the interactive channels and satellite links can be established in classrooms through dial up PCTC lines and use of analog TV and audio channels can be made for distance education. V-set in working system can be used for teaching, research, extension and training in distantly situated class rooms by combining digitally controlled TV with distant training software in the following two manners:

(a) Online education delivery.
(b) Offline data entry system for declaring syllabi, advertisements, applications, registration and examination control.

TDMA and DAMA V-SAT system can be used for interactive distance education through digital TV communications.

Worldwide education on the Internet is marketed and sold on its interactive uniqueness. Course materials are prepared and posted on the sites of teaching schools or the universities and the enrolled students are given access. Students can post doubts to the lecturers using e-mail. The greatest advantage is peer-group introduction in which the students can chat with other with or without monitoring by a lecturer. Majority of courses offered online are those related to the development. These online courses are taken mostly in urban areas attached to the Internet in some way or the other.

(c) Internet-Telephony

It consists of three key technologies:

(i) Internet Protocol (IP),
(ii) Asynchronous transfer mode (ATM), and
(iii) Frame-delay (FD).

Even if your friend does not have a computer with PC-to-phone Internet Telephone, you can call any telephone number right from your desk-top. Your call is carried over the Internet to a "gateway" where it is converted between the NET and the standard telephony network. This Internet-telephony will boom with its only Rs. 2/- per minute charge irrespective of distance. With this facility even a very common man will have telephonic connectivity with anywhere in the whole world almost without spending any money for this call.

(d) High-Tech Medical Instruments

Use of the computer and information technology would ensure the revolution in the field of healthcare, medical science and family welfare for common masses of the society. By the use of electronics in stethoscope, it would be capable of amplifying biological sounds up to 14 times higher than the conventional stethoscope to help clinical doctor in detecting heart and lung problems. Suitable medical software can be developed for computerization of diagnosing process with upmost accuracy and also for giving correct prescriptions of medicines to cure such diagnostics problems. In the field of neurology, the methods of neurocomputing can be very helpful.

(e) Digital Libraries

In the age of very fast growth of knowledge in every branch and the consequent publications of large number of new books, periodicals and research journals in each field, it is becoming almost impossible for any standard library to procure, secure and maintain the whole available relevant literature in these fields of knowledge. As such, it is becoming necessary to collect all academic information by Internet connectivity and store them in the form of computer floppies so that any relevant portion can be reproduced (down loaded) as and when needed by the user.

Negative Effects of Computer and Information Technologies

In spite of continuous expanding scope of utility of computers and information technologies in almost every sphere of human life, their fast developing techniques are sending alarming signals also for safeguarding the human values, cultural heritage, ethical environment and spiritual atmosphere of our society. In India, we have our moral values, spiritual standards and pure social structure which our ancestors had always preserved in spite of the fact that science had first flourished long ago in our country. In the attempts to understand nature in terms of process and constitutes, ancient Indian philosophers went much beyond the world of sensory appearance and relying upon rational analysis free from direct observational contents they could visualize symmetries, structure of matter, commune evolution, expanding universe as analyzed in *Vaishesic* and *Sankhya darshans* and all the four *Vedas*. The balance had been maintained between materialism and idealism, consumerism and spiritualism, and between manifested world and the unmanifested one. We always had the path in controlling and regularizing Arth and *Kama* by *Dharma* to achieve the ultimate goal of *Moksha*. In spite of foreign rules for several hundred years, Indians did not let lose their cultural heritage, moral values, social structure and rich traditions. But the recent revolution of various TV channels, interconnectivity, computers and information technology is rapidly polluting our civilisation, rich traditions, high moral value system and spiritual faiths through various such programmes which are not socially acceptable, morally ethical and culturally rich.

Besides these serious risks involved in the free use of computers and information technology, there are many other negative impacts of those techniques on human values of a civilised society. Some of them are as below:

(a) Hi-Tech Cheating

Using the ultra fast communicating devices like IT and the increasing capacity of rapidly getting faster super computers, the evil brains of destructive approaches are coming up with new devices of cheating, deceiving, robbing and creating new scams at individual, national and international levels in the fields of banking, business, politics, science, trading and sex crimes. Before the significant development of those high-tech techniques of computers and IT, there was a burning news in 70's that a cheat could draw a huge amount of money from national bank in the name of the then prime minister of India, Mrs. Indira Gandhi, by changing his voice on telephone. We can very well imagine to what extent these new high-tech devices can be misused for huge cheating if the simple use of ordinary telephone could lead to such a notorious bank scam in the seventh decade.

(b) Virtual Nudity

The technique of virtual reality in three-dimensional picture using computer and information technology is being misused in western world to develop dirty, unseeingly immoral methods of harassment of women by superimposing the actual face of one woman on the nude body of another woman. There have been reports of the demonstration of virtual rapes on some woman by the use of these techniques. The scenes of vulgarity, rudeness and violence in movies are rapidly increasing diving immoral and ethically objectionable messages to the young boys and girls of the civilized society.

(c) Hi-Tech Culture as Master

These rapid communication techniques and new experiences and computers are drastically changing the world culture, and day by day we are becoming slaves of these technologies. In old education system, a lot of efforts were made to sharpen the memory of students and they were trained to effectively express their original views by combining them with knowledge stored in their brains. Such old education system was being used to prepare students to be good orators and excellent speakers in the all fields of knowledge and all walks of life. But, with the fast expanding uses of these hi-tech devices, our students are becoming completely dependent on these techniques with no opportunity left for original thinking, innovative ideas and constructive planning. As such, these hi-tech devices are adversely effecting our work culture.

(d) Risk of Increasing Unemployment

Rapidly increasing the use of computers and information technology in administrative offices, banks, post offices, libraries, distance education, internal training programme etc. is creating the risk of retrenchments of staff and employees in all these organisations. The American culture of "hire and fire" is being adopted in other countries also by using these devices. The less needed or not needed person can be informed by a simple message on e-mail rather personally telling him. This fastly expanding culture will adversely effect the job opportunities and increase the risk of more and more unemployment among youths.

Besides the above adversities, the continuous use of computers and information technology may lead to eye problems, strains and neurological problems among youths.

22

Impact of Information Technology on Society

A.S. Patil

Information technology such as computers, satellite T.V. channels, mobile, iridium technology is that for which the world is breathing today. It will be the factor that will introduce mankind to the 21st century. With all the technological advancements that are being made in this area to ease human life, one should not overlook the serious consequences which will cost us in terms of human values. Technology, as it is universally accepted, is a boon to mankind to make life an easy affair. To eliminate the brutal and hazardous working conditions, where exploitation of working class was a common affair, computers are providing necessary intelligence and cheaper solutions. In other words, the computer technology is controlling mechanical devices used in places like coal mines, oil wells, atomic reactors, etc.

With the help of television channels, every individual today is aware of his rights and duties towards the society. People are motivated to think and act due to the short programmes like serials and panel discussions on burning topics such as dowry, child labour, illiteracy, AIDS, supersititions, national integration, etc. These discussions are watched by millions of people all over the world. There is no other medium than information technology that could communicate these to many individuals at a time. Information technology, therefore, can be defined as a 'technology world without borders'. The Internet spanning the globe is engulfing whichever organisation or individual comes in its way. It provides a platform for masses to discuss on various different issues from arts to science, superstitions, alcoholism, etc. People are being attacked by the media, and a solution to every query is provided by chat and newsgroup. Computers are being used as mouthpieces to chat or communicate with persons online. Statistics say that about 150 million people throughout the world are using Internet. Experts estimate that 5 million more come online every month. That is a single piece of information broadcasted, is immediately available to many persons at a time. Most of the human oriented systems are being computerized with computing power that is harnessed to its maximum extent. With newly emerging technologies like multimedia, virtual reality, video conferencing, cyber cafe, cyber clubs, DVDs etc., a jungle of technology is created where a human cannot make out where he or she really is. Kids today are playing video/computer games, and surfing the Internet. Today, their ideas are for superheroes like *Shaktiman*, Captain Wyom, Bill Gates, Akshay Kumar, and Madhuri Dixit instead of Nehru, Gandhi and Abraham Lincoln. These kids and teenagers are no longer lured by "The Daffodils" of William Wordsworth, but by the MP3 versions of audio-video ablums available on the Internet. Students are trying to imitate the cyber heroes that they see in all sorts of games available. Just to quote a story of two eleven-grade students, who fired on their fellow classmates and teachers just for the sake of adventure shattered not only you and us but also the whole world. It is also known that these students later on committed suicide. Where did these students learn to use weapons, kill people, commit suicide? The computer games such as Wolf3D etc. are acting as simulator programme in killing people. Where, on the other hand, simulator programmes are used on a computer to train a pilot both saving his life and the plane from a possible crash. We have read also about a site that teaches how to open locks without keys. Is this necessary?.

There is a competition between channels and sites to provide the latest information and, on the part of the surfers, they are demanding for more and more updates. In the run of collecting the latest information, the paparazzi killed lady

Diana. Distribution of pornographic material all over the Internet is reaching its height in which not only adults but also teenagers and children are involved. Wrong and inhumane information on such topics is damaging the cultures that most of the countries have cherished since generations. We all know about the deformation of a famous heroine whose photograph was deformed with some model and was presented in an objectionable form and made available on the internet for millions to view. But these current dangers on the Internet are far less than reported and even further less than that one faces everyday in public places where the walls are painted depicting all sorts of nonsense, objectionable books sold on the footpath, etc. In a discussion on the question about pornography on the web and how to protect innocent students, people round the world suggested that the solution was providing good literature, good drama, fine arts and education of the type that will encourage youth to distinguish right from wrong.

It is clear that electronic medium is impacting on the way that human proceses information, but in many ways, the electronic medium is restoring ancient traditions of story telling, reviving ancient languages and bringing generations closer together. Many families are scanning old photographs of the deceased relatives and using computer networks to chronicle and write down family history. Many children are using computer networks to ask senior citizens the questions about what life was like when they were young. Many college students and their parents are using computer networks to maintain daily communication when separated by physical distance.

Wisdom is not solely a by-product of reading. Surely before Gothenberg, people were wise. Wisdom is, however, the desire to find truth, and that search might bridge generation and historical periods. It is due to IT that through communication, co-operation and collaboration, wisdom is being put forth to promote our common heritage and humanity. A majority of entrepreneurs, who are taking to home computing as their business, are those who believe they can be more productive and creative if they could create a workplace in the comfort of their own home. But this has a downside that you cannot get away from work while you are always near it. This always will pave way to damage the marital relationship and also parent-child relationship. On the positive front, a working mother needs not leave her kid in the day-care centre, if her work is totally confined to the Internet.

Many of the physically handicapped being blind or visually impaired or suffering from learning disability like dyslexia now can use computers. Systems like ARIA are developed for such people in which blinds with knowledge of Braille will be able to use computers with the help of Perkins keyboard and even to get a normal English as well as a Braille printout by the ARIA Embosser. By using the Embosser attached to such a computer, the blinds too can share the information that is available worldwide. Although the above is a very good example of computers assisting in learning, one should not overlook that exposure to the electronic mediums are certainly harming both physiologically and psychologically to the young learners as we have stated earlier.

It is found that people are getting addicted to the glamour posed by these technologies, and possession of Internet account, computer, cellular phones, etc. are taken as a status symbol. It was expected that crimes would be reduced with the help of information technology. But it is not so; by software piracy one gets unwanted electronic matter posted in his inbox, frauds related to telegraphic transfers, breaking into the system, hacking the remote machines, playing with web site information stored by others are examples of e-crimes (Electronic Crimes), as we call it. New laws are required to deal with it. Ads on these kinds of media are not controlled and are popularizing smoking, drinking and other kinds of vices. Most of the registered e-mail users' inbox also contain e-mails from prostitutes all over the world from countries like Spain, Germany and France explaining unwanted statistics. Where, on the other hand, you have sites of social movements like Prajapita Brahmakumari giving you the messages of divine/ virtues. Education imparted by distance learning *e.g.*, the IGNOU is one such institution, which is imparting distance education. In projects like "Warna Wired Village Project", IT is helping mankind by establishing the relation of computers and information technology with agriculture. We know about some satellite channels that telecast some objectionable serials that should be banned from viewing in some parts of the world where the culture is of a different kind.

Information technology is having a deep impact on the lives of growing number of people around the world. It is offering the possibility of significant positive social and personal growth, but only to those who use it reasonably and effectively in their normal life, and not lose the bottomlines. It can provide productive learning in schools and a full and satisfying life for the individual, or collaborative and cooperative communities of learners for the global society. It also seems appropriate to use information technology and computers to deal with human issues raised by itself.

At last, we should not forget the fundamental principle about information technology which is to provide information to most of those people in the world, who are committed to democracy, volunteerism and a professional code of honour, that is based on co-operation and collaboration rather than corruption and competition.

References

Herman, Tanvi, "The Future of Computing and Quality of Life", *IS World Net*.

Home Page, *www.reconnecting.com*.

Kathy, Ruthkowski, A Childhood Remebered: The Magic of Computer Networks, *www.chaos.com/netteach*.

Kathy, Ruthkowski, "The Fate of Wisdom in Electronic Age", *www.chaos.com/netteach*.

Kathy, Ruthkowski, "To Build a Wall or to Build Values — That is the Question", *www.chaos.com/netteach*.

Venkatramaiah , S.R. and K. Sreenivasa Rao (1992), *Science Technology and Social Development*, DPH.

Index